VANISHING IRELAND

Friendship and Community

VANISHING IRELAND

Friendship and Community

JAMES FENNELL AND TURTLE BUNBURY

HACHETTE
BOOKS
IRELAND

To my mother Lesley Fennell, with thanks for everything, love James

To dear Rosebud, thanks for being such a cool aunt, love Turtle

Copyright © 2013 photographs, James Fennell
Copyright © 2013 text, Turtle Bunbury

First published in 2013 by Hachette Books Ireland
An Hachette UK Company

1

ISBN 978 1444 733068

Typeset in Garamond by Anú Design, Tara
Cover and text design by Anú Design, Tara
Printed and bound in Great Britain by Butler Tanner and Dennis Ltd

Hachette Books Ireland policy is to use papers that are natural, renewable and recyclable products and made from
wood grown in sustainable forests. The logging and manufacturing processes are expected to conform to the
environmental regulations of the country of origin.

Hachette Books Ireland
8 Castlecourt Centre
Castleknock
Dublin 15
Ireland

A division of Hachette UK, 338 Euston Road, London NW1 3BH, England
www.hachette.ie

Introduction

In August 1858, one of the most remarkable feats in the history of global engineering was achieved when the Atlantic Cable Company connected a cable linking Valentia Island in County Kerry to Heart's Content in Newfoundland. The US President James Buchanan, whose father hailed from County Donegal, dispatched an ecstatic message down the cable to Queen Victoria declaring the transatlantic link to be 'a triumph more glorious and far more useful to mankind than any battle'. It was his great hope that the link would 'prove to be a bond of perpetual peace and friendship between the kindred nations, and an instrument destined by Divine Providence to diffuse religion, civilization, liberty, and law throughout the world'.

It took seventeen hours for President Buchanan's message to get down the wire. But when it arrived, the Western world went into throes of jubilant ecstasy. Church bells rang across Ireland, England and America. One hundred cannons saluted the New York skies. Streets were bedecked with flags. It was all deeply exciting and revolutionary.

And then, about two weeks later, the cable stopped working and the revolution subsided. It took seven years to fix the cable – think about that next time your broadband goes down. But fix it they did and the shimmering new 1866 cable from Ireland to the USA could transmit messages at a super-zippy eight words a minute.

The importance of the transatlantic connection between Ireland and North America was phenomenal. Prior to the telegraph, a message took approximately ten days to cross the Atlantic because the only possible carrier was a ship. Now you could send a message from the Old World to the New World within minutes. An entire community evolved around the three transatlantic cable stations that were built in southwest Kerry to accommodate this new industry, and the people of Ballinskelligs provide the basis of a chapter in this book.

In 1902, the transatlantic cable was superseded when the Italian-Irish inventor Guglielmo Marconi transmitted a wireless message across the Atlantic from Connemara to Glace Bay, Nova Scotia in Canada. The impact of Marconi's pioneering visit to Galway is still being felt over a hundred years later, as we discovered when we interviewed the people of Connemara for this book.

Connemara was also the destination for the next gigantic link between Ireland and North America. In June 1919, Captain John Alcock and Lieutenant Arthur Whitten Brown completed the first non-stop transatlantic flight between America and Europe. The utterly fearless duo flew in an open-cockpit Vimy, which meant that every time they passed through a band of rain, hail, sleet or snow – which they did frequently – it 'chewed bits out of our faces', to quote Brown. When their plane safely crash-landed onto a bog near Clifden, the world once again celebrated as the older generations reeled in amazement. The voyage to America had always taken weeks. Yet this flying machine had done it in sixteen hours.

We've come a long way, no doubts. The cable, the radio and the aeroplane were all stepping stones that made this world of ours so small that even the remote wilds of Ireland's Atlantic coast could no longer hide from the evolution of the global community. It will be hard, if not impossible, for my two small daughters to imagine that people once lived without mobile phones, remote controls and high-speed broadband – developments that should be embraced for their immense ability to enhance our lives.

I am particularly excited to think that we are moving into an age when it will be completely normal for our elders to communicate with their geographically distant children and grandchildren by email, Facebook, Skype and whatever new forms of communication come our way, as well as 'old-fashioned' face-to-face encounters. Likewise, as people gain a better understanding of how to use technology, the possibilities it affords to the sick, the aged, the lonely and the bored could and should be profoundly uplifting.

And yet I also feel a massive tug for those who cannot adjust to this new world. I think of my late grandfather who, born in 1910, reckoned that the Ireland of his childhood was little different to that which had existed for hundreds of years. Fields were tilled by man, horse and plough. Seeds were scattered by hand. Crops were harvested by sickle and scythe. The community united to help with the harvest. Birds twittered in every hedgerow and church bells rang when the harvest was complete.

For my grandfather, the villain of the piece was hydraulics. They paved the way for the tractor that so rudely shoved the workhorse into the hedge. Likewise, the combine harvester, which could do in an hour what an entire community could achieve in a day. Or the robotic sprayers who roamed the land, suffocating birds and insects with their poisonous fumes. My grandfather was appalled by such things but he understood that sometimes to achieve what we believe to be progress, other things must take a hit.

Not everyone mourned the passing of the old world. There were plenty who loved the idea of a tractor with the pulling power of a team of workhorses. No need for daily harnessing and endless hay. No anxieties for the animals in bad weather. Simply hop up in the tractor seat, twist the key and you're away.

As we advance into the future, we will no doubt lament the manner in which we are obliged to leave certain aspects of our past behind in deference to progress. The pace of life continues to accelerate so that we no longer give one another the time of day, as we did in decades past. So perhaps we should take a deep breath to relish the things we enjoyed in the past.

Life is all about magic moments and trying to make them last as long as possible. We do that best when we are in the company of others. Making eye contact and exchanging banter, sharing crummy jokes and tall stories, gossip, memories, recipes, hardships, adventures, childhoods, melancholy, laughter. We interact because humans thrive on friendship. In decades past, we formed communities because we worked better as a pack.

Our sense of community is under threat. The disconnection between neighbours is palpable. Disappointing as it may be, it is an inevitable consequence of a society that lives within increasingly private comfort zones.

Maybe things will come full circle. I once met an elderly farmer called Dan Mackey at the Harp Inn in Ballitore, County Kildare. 'You might call me mad,' he said, 'but, I'm telling you now, the wheel will keep turning and the horse and cart will be back.'

Turtle Bunbury

Ellen O'Keeffe,
Timmy O'Keeffe & Patsy Kingston

Caherlaska, County Cork

Housewife, Farmer & Farmer, Soldier and Bus Driver

Born 1920, 1931 & 1935

In the late 1890s, Denis O'Keeffe of Caherlaska sold fourteen acres for £7, gathered up his family and set off on the 110-kilometre trek to Queenstown (now Cobh) to take an emigrant ship to America. When they arrived at Queenstown, the O'Keeffes discovered that the fare had gone up. They would have to leave one of their daughters behind.

'My grandfather had to go down and bring the child back,' says Timmy O'Keeffe. 'He had to carry her all the way. Every time he left her down, she would stay put until he came back and picked her up again.'

This heart-breaking story gains some relief when we learn that the girl's family later sent over the fare for her passage and she did eventually join them. Many decades on, two of her daughters returned to Ireland and visited the home of their forbears, which Timmy's father was by then using as a storehouse for turnips.

This tale is relayed to us while we sit in Timmy's living room, the turf smouldering in the burner, with Timmy in one armchair, his neighbour Patsy Kingston in another and a sheepdog called Lassie ambling in between.

Timmy is the older man by a few years. They have been friends since childhood, despite the complications of one being Protestant and the other Catholic. 'He went that way to school and I went that way,' explains Patsy, and the two men laugh rumbustiously for a moment or two.

The townland of Caherlaska, where they live, lies on a headland just west of Schull in west Cork, overlooking the choppy Celtic Sea. The name Cathair Leasca translates as 'stone fort of the Duibh Leasc', although locals also refer to it as 'the burned city', after a village that stood here until it was deliberately burned to the ground during an outbreak of the deadly cholera.

The O'Keeffes have been here a long time. The 1901 census clocked Timmy's great-grandfather, Daniel O'Keeffe, as an eighty-eight-year-old Catholic farmer who spoke both English and Irish but who could not read. The two-room house where he lived is now a shed.

Opposite page: Timmy O'Keeffe.

Timmy lives in a house built in 1920 by his grandfather 'Old Thady' O'Keeffe who had secured funding for the construction through one of the last grants given out by the British government. Thady and his wife, Mary, had an arranged marriage. 'That was standard practice,' says Timmy. 'People didn't get much option to marry for love.'

The marriage produced five children, all of whom later emigrated to Boston or Brooklyn, except Timmy's father, John.

Amongst the O'Keeffes who remained in Caherlaska was Timmy's cousin, Jeremiah O'Keeffe, a farmer. In 1945, Jeremiah married Ellen Wilcox who, now in her ninety-fourth year, still lives at Caherlaska with her son, Billy, and his wife, Mary. Ellen was actually born in New Bedford, Massachusetts, in 1920 where her father William Wilcox, an Irish émigré, worked in the gasworks. Shortly after Ellen's fifth birthday, William inherited a farm west of Goleen in County Cork from a cousin, so he left his job and returned to Ireland with his wife and children. The final leg of the voyage home took place in a storm and Ellen can still recall the sound of someone on the ship shouting, 'There's land! Look! Look at it!'

Ellen's mother died in 1932, after complications giving birth to a daughter, during the very same week that Ellen was to be confirmed. A fluent Irish speaker, Ellen was initially called to train as a teacher but ultimately married Jeremiah and moved to Caherlaska where her six children were born and raised.

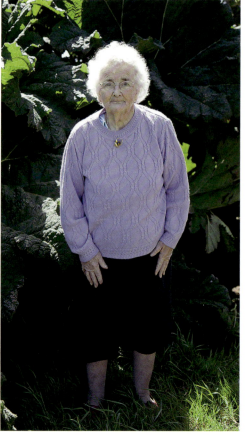

Her Wilcox ancestors descend from a shipwrecked sailor who came ashore in Ballycotton and went to work for 'the Pirate Hull' in Leamcon. Sir William Hull, the shady Vice-Admiral of Munster, was supposed to prevent piracy along this stretch of the Irish coast. Instead, he joined in the fun, converting Leamcon into a hub for the pirates of the North Atlantic and making a tidy fortune from the illicit cargos that passed him by. 'Briseann an dúchais trí shúile an chait,' remarks Ellen. 'Nature breaks out through the eyes of the cat.'

Patsy Kingston knows all about the Pirate Hull. The farmhouse where he lives looks directly across to Hull's

Top: Timmy O'Keeffe. Bottom: Ellen O'Keeffe. Opposite page: Patsy Kingston.

stone castle at Leamcon. Patsy's ancestor, Colonel James Kingston, was, like Hull, an Englishman. He served in the army of William of Orange and apparently once gave King Billy the use of his own horse for which he and his family were given substantial lands on the Beara Peninsula. These included a farm just west of Drimoleague where Patsy's grandfather, Allen Kingston, was born.

Patsy's mother, Katy Pyburn, had gone to Chicago as a young woman and struck lucky when she encountered a disgruntled cousin of the Wrigley family who was looking for a new nanny. She spent the next eleven years working in well-to-do Lake Forest in Illinois, where she also managed to secure jobs for three of her sisters. When her brother was bankrupted by the 1929 Wall Street Crash, she took him back to Ireland where she rekindled a romance with her childhood sweetheart, Sam Kingston. She then returned to the USA for three more years while Sam concentrated on farming – 'and smoking his pipe,' laughs Patsy. They exchanged letters regularly, although Patsy adds that his father was receiving similar letters from 'a few more girlfriends as well at that time!' Finally, the couple married and settled on the farm in Caherlaska where Patsy was born.

As a child, Patsy sometimes hitched a lift to school on his father's donkey and trap. This enabled him to compete with his neighbour, Timmy O'Keeffe, who consistently managed to grab a ride to his Irish-speaking school at Lowertown on the creamery cart as it passed by.

The Economic War with England was ongoing during their childhood but, while times were tough, Timmy reckons it wasn't so bad. 'There was no money but people had no mortgages to pay, no overheads, no headaches. Not like they do now. They were able to live off the land. They only went to town for tea and sugar. But there was no sport around here only milking cows! Three cows before you went into school in the morning.'

'We were hardy lads then,' agrees Patsy. 'You weren't sitting down, twisting a wheel all day like the farmers are now. It was all manual labour, piking hay and corn. It all had to be handled. Even the men who worked in the docks did everything by hand.'

Patsy always yearned to travel and in 1953, the eighteen-year-old emigrated to Gloucester in England, where he found work conducting and then driving double-decker buses. 'I was eight miles from Cheltenham,' says Patsy, who enjoys horse-racing. 'And that's the best way you can explain it to an Irishman.'

As a bus driver, he was liable for two years' national service and so, in 1959, he was assigned to the Royal Irish Fusiliers and dispatched to their base in Armagh. The following year, he was sent with the North Irish Brigade to Libya where he drove lorries and ambulances up and down the border. The man in charge of one of the border posts was a young Bedouin by name of Muammar al-Gaddafi.

'He was a very sulky man,' says Patsy. 'I said to my mates that if ever there's to be a coup in this place, he'll be the fecker who leads it.'

While in Tripoli, Patsy and his fellow soldiers also hosted the 33rd Battalion of the Irish army while they acclimatised before their deployment to the Congo. 'They only had their heavy Irish uniforms which they'd have dropped dead in, so we gave them our tropical kit.'

He left the army soon after, having turned down an opportunity to train as an officer. After seventeen years away, he returned to Ireland to take on the seventy-five-acre farm after the premature death of his younger brother Edward. The woman he was with at the time stayed back in England.

'And I never married either, but I was lucky to keep myself,' says Timmy. He had remained in west Cork throughout Patsy's absence, save for a three-month stint as a builder and farm labourer in Bedfordshire, England.

Now considered one of the wisest farmers in the area, Timmy is utterly familiar with every horse and cow, breed, seed and generation. But he would not like to have driven a double-decker bus. 'I never even drove a car,' says he. 'A bicycle and a Ferguson 20 tractor were good for me.'

He often took the tractor down to Colla House, a small hotel nearby where he would sometimes sing a ballad or two. The hotel sadly closed in 2000 – as have nearly half of the sixteen pubs in Schull – although he still calls into The Bunratty on a Friday afternoon.

'You could go down to Schull in the old days at any time and you'd meet someone in a pub,' says he. 'Now most of them don't open until the evening and there is no one there except at the weekends. It was a different class of people back then. When the Celtic Tiger came, everything went mad and that finished it altogether. I wonder will the good times return? They would want to come fairly fast, I suppose.'

Jimmy Murphy

Ballinskelligs, County Kerry

Farmer

Born 1951

'That was a fresh breeze last night,' says Jimmy Murphy.

This is something of an understatement. I'd been on Bolus Head for five nights and already survived three thunderstorms. The one to which Jimmy is referring, the most recent, was also the most powerful. The cottage where I was staying was pitched just one small, scraggly field away from the storm-battered shore. In the midst of the storm, I ventured outside to contemplate the sheer pulsating power of the Atlantic breakers rolling in from the west, smashing into the cliffs around me. Here, on the most westerly reaches of the Kingdom of Kerry, it felt like we were in for the most ferocious storm in Irish history since the Night of the Big Wind tore across the island in 1839.

The storm died down over the course of the night. The sinister grey skies and tempestuous waves disappeared. A series of large green forms emerged warily from the haze. Scariff Island. Deenish Island. Derrynane, with the Beara Peninsula rippling beyond. And, in the foreground, Ballinskelligs Bay, into whose dark blue waters the sons of Milesius sailed their ships long centuries before written records.

The sense of history is powerful. It's in the remnants of the beehive huts scattered in the rocks. It's in the sandstone coral and the ancient potato ridges that lie utterly camouflaged amid the stone-strewn landscape until you stare closely at the maze of green and grey and gradually begin to distinguish the secrets of the past. Small wonder that Ballinskelligs, or *Baile an Sceilg*, translates as 'homestead of the rocks'.

A Napoleonic lookout post is silhouetted on the horizon. Beneath it sprawls a whitewashed farmhouse with the ruins of two older buildings adjacent. As I pass by the farmhouse, a sable collie bounds out. 'Shhhhhhkip,' hails a voice from the doorway, and the collie screeches to a cartoon-like halt.

And that's how I met Jimmy Murphy. He came out to say hello and we stood talking by a mountain stream that rushed under the ground beneath us. The sky was vast and blue, the ocean serene. Jimmy's family have lived here for hundreds of years. They built the walls around us. He pointed out the timber and wire fences that separate the fields, each designating different plots assigned to different families by the Land Commission a century ago. Some fields slope gently down to the shoreline. Others plunge over the cliffs into the ocean beneath.

'My farm goes all the way to Bolus Head,' explained Jimmy. 'They say this is the end of the world.'

You can see why. The road to Bolus Head stops at Jimmy's farmhouse. If you keep west, the next stop is Newfoundland in Canada.

When Jimmy was a child, his father reared cattle and horses on this land. Jimmy helped him from an early age. One brother went to England, another to Dublin and a sister lives in nearby Caherciveen. Jimmy never left. 'There was plenty of work on the farms around here in those days,' he says. 'And there was plenty of money too.' He learned to drive in a Ford Prefect when he was fifteen years old, but has rarely ventured beyond Kerry's borders. He sometimes visits his brother in Dublin but has yet to leave Ireland. 'I might leave yet but, if I do, I may never come back,' he laughs.

In 1966, he took over the farm and switched to sheep, homing in on the Texas sheep that are now scattered high and low above the road.

'This would have been a difficult place in times past for sure,' he acknowledged. 'They were tough people. They weren't sitting up on high stools in bars. They might have had a bit of poitín for Christmas. And they smoked – the women too, smoking the pipe – but t'was the only pleasure they had, I suppose. We've come a long way since. Whether it's for better or worse, I don't know. Humans are always complaining. And maybe they were complaining a hundred years ago too.'

As our conversation ended, Jimmy bade me farewell and set off into the upper fields, a man with a mission. 'I've to fetch a sheep for the butcher,' he explained. Whatever that entails.

Ballinskelligs, County Kerry

Micheál Ó Braonáin (Storyteller and Electrician, born 1956),

Willie Joe Cronin (Farmer, born 1956), Christy Kate O'Sullivan (Farmer, born 1951),

Tom Horgan (Weather Observer, born 1938),

Joe C. Keating (Builder and Salvage Expert, born 1931)

My base in County Kerry was one of the charming stone cottages overlooking Ballinskelligs Bay at Cill Rialaig. Threatened with demolition, this row of nine cottages was a veritable ruin when it was salvaged and resurrected as an artists' and writers' retreat by Noelle Campbell-Sharp in 1991.

One hundred years ago, these same cottages were home to a small community of Irish-speakers including the renowned storyteller, or *seanchaí*, Seán Ó Conaill.

I learned a good deal about Seán Ó Conaill when I met his great-grandnephew, Micheál Ó Braonáin, at a wake in Cable O'Leary's pub in Ballinskelligs. A popular lady called Eileen O'Sullivan had been buried that morning so most of the community were gathered in the pub for soup, sandwiches and liquid refreshments. As Ballinskelligs is part of the Gaeltacht, much of the banter was *as gaeilge* but there are fears that widespread usage of the Irish language is endangered even here on the coast of southwest Kerry.

Micheál told me that the houses at Cill Rialaig were originally built in the late eighteenth century by Geoffrey Ó Conaill, who is believed to have been a great-grandfather of Seán the *seanchaí*. Geoffrey grew up at Baslickane, near Waterville, on land owned by Maurice 'Hunting Cap' O'Connell, an uncle of Daniel O'Connell, the Catholic Emancipator. However, disaster struck when Maurice was arrested for smuggling and given a stark choice. 'He was told he must either face the wrath of the courts or give up his lands at Baslickane,' says Micheál gravely. 'He chose to give up his lands and Geoffrey Ó Conaill had to leave.'

A few generations later, Seán Ó Conaill emerged as one of the Iveragh Peninsula's finest storytellers. His wife, Cáit, shared his passion and was always on hand to help steer him back on track if he lost his way mid-story. The couple came into their element in 1923 when seventy-year-old Seán became muse to a twenty-four-year-old historian, Séamus Ó Duilearga. A native of the Glens of Antrim, Ó Duilearga had come to the area to collect Irish folklore – old songs, old stories, proverbs and sayings.

Ó Duilearga returned to Ballinskelligs every year for the next seven years to talk with the illiterate and completely uneducated Ó Conaill. Having grown up in an age when storytellers were abundant across Kerry, Ó Conaill completely understood the nature and importance of Ó Duilearga's mission. The age of the *seanchaí* was drawing to a close.

Opposite page: Micheál Ó Braonáin.

The two men were rarely alone. Ó Conaill's house was a *tigh bothántaíochta*, or rambling house, into which anything up to a dozen people would gather around the fireside by night. They were generally neighbours, drawn by the excitement of a stranger in the area, and often fine storytellers in their own right. By the time of Ó Conaill's death in 1931, Ó Duilearga had gathered what is regarded as one of the greatest collections ever provided by a storyteller.

'And so it proved the *béaloideas* [folklore] never dies,' says Micheál. 'People move on a generation but the *béaloideas* lives forever.'

Micheál has retained the storyteller's gift, elongating paragraphs with considerable eloquence. No detail is too trivial and he shows a deft knowledge of global history from the wilds of the American frontiers to the convict settlements of Australia and back to the desperate days of the eighteenth century when the British Redcoats were on the prowl all across the Iveragh.

The storytelling tradition was still strong in the 1950s Ireland of Micheál's youth, particularly in the house of his grandparents, Ned and Mary Lawlor. Ned's life story was a dramatic one from the moment he became involved with Cable O'Leary himself – this powerful Ballinskelligs man had been born Donncha O'Leary, but acquired his nickname because he single-handedly saved the Atlantic cable from disaster in the mid-1880s. However, his heroism did not prevent the local sheriff and his bailiffs from evicting the O'Learys from their homestead in 1894. Ned, a teenager at the time, took an active role in helping O'Leary resist the constabulary. 'He picked stones out of the river for Cable O'Leary to shell the Peelers with,' explains Micheál.

Ultimately, Cable O'Leary had to yield to the law and abandon his home, sealing his iconic status in the region. Shortly afterwards, Ned emigrated to America, with three of his brothers, and remained there until 1910, helping to lay railway tracks across New England and Connecticut.

Opposite page: Joe C. Keating (left),
with friend John Joe O'Sullivan (right).

Ned was working in Flannery's Bar in Hartford, Connecticut, when he met his future wife Mary Ó Conaill, a niece of Seán the *seanchaí*. They subsequently returned to Kerry and lived the rest of their lives near Ballinskelligs. Their daughter, Eileen, was Micheál's mother, a psychiatric nurse who, as her son marvels, 'could nearly tell you what you were thinking before you thought it'.

Amongst Ned's contemporaries were Mike and Noreen Corcoran who lived at Cloghaneanua, just north of Ballinskelligs. Their grandson, Willie Joe Cronin, gave me an insight into their lives. 'My grandfather was blind for twenty-two years with the glaucoma. He worked hard in the bogs, cutting turf, milking cows, trying to bring up a family of four children. They had no money to develop the land or anything. At night, they would sit down beside a big fire, with turf or bog oak burning, and they were as happy there as anywhere. Smoking the old clay pipes and having a chat. My grandfather would put the tobacco into his mouth and suck the juice out of it. That's the way they got on in life. It was tough, but they got through it. They hadn't the price of drink but they were happy at that time.'

Set dancing was a regular pastime in the Cronin house. 'I'm shovelling up on sixty years old but I remember the dancing well on the old stone floors. There were no timber floors that time. Clackety clack. With the hard shoes, the shoemaker's shoes, made for the job. Bang, bang, clackety clack. Everyone played music then. Or else they sang. Republican songs mostly. We're big Republicans around here.'

Christy Kate O'Sullivan, a local farmer, is amongst those who kept the musical tradition going strong. A devotee of the 'top class' accordionist Bernie Moran of Sussa, Christy played the very same instrument 'until my fingers got so bent and crooked I had to stop'. As a young man, Christy was one of hundreds who crossed the Irish Sea to work in the beet factories of Felsted in Essex for four seasons. 'You'd start at seven in the morning and go until three,' he recalls. 'Or else you'd take the shift from three until eleven at night. The factory never stopped. The beet factories were very good to the Irish people. There were not many from the short-grass counties like Kildare and Meath, but there were a huge crowd from the poorer counties, Kerry and Donegal, Mayo and Galway. We were all speaking *as gaeilge* but it might have been the Connemara Irish and the Donegal Irish or even the Tourmakeady Irish.'

One of the lesser known of southwest Kerry's manifold charms are its nocturnal vistas of the star-filled skies. The almost total absence of light pollution provides spectacular views on clear, dark nights. One man who knows all about this is Tom Horgan, who has spent some thirty years reporting on the region's weather by day and night. Tom grew up on a small farm outside of Tralee where he was one of eight children. As a boy, he realised the farming life was not for him. 'We had the grass for ten cows and the water for a hundred.'

In 1958, the twenty-year-old farmer's son arrived in Caherciveen to work at the Meteorological Observatory. 'I came by train on the rail line that closed two years later. It was my first time south of Killorglin and I found it very different. Cars were scarce on the roads. Many still travelled by horse and carts. There were donkeys and people walking and bicycling everywhere. But it was very friendly here and there was a strong sense of community, which I took to very much.'

Tom subsequently married and settled in Waterville from where he commuted to the Caherciveen weather station until he took early retirement in 1988. Together with his wife, Mary, and their family, he also operated Waterville Caravan & Camping Park from 1977 to 2000.

While in Waterville, he developed his curiosity for local heritage, particularly the story of the Atlantic cable. The first transatlantic telegraph cable was laid in 1858 from Valentia Island to Heart's Content in Newfoundland, but only worked for a few weeks. Seven years later, the first commercially successful cable was laid by the Anglo-American Telegraph Company along the same route. A message could be sent at eight

Opposite page: Willie Joe Cronin. Previous spread: Christy Kate O'Sullivan (left), Joe C. Keating (right).

words a minute. A second cable was laid down by Siemens in 1874 and ran from Ballinskelligs Bay to Torbay, Nova Scotia. In 1884, things moved on apace when Cyrus Field's Commercial Cable Company laid another transatlantic cable from Waterville to Canso, Nova Scotia.

The three cable stations had a huge impact on southwest Kerry. Waterville became a boom town, with nearly three hundred workers at the cable station through until the 1950s. 'Nearly half of them were English or Scottish,' says Tom. 'And they had their families there too. Some said Waterville was the most English town in Ireland.'

The Ballinskelligs station closed in 1923. By the mid-1960s, satellites and new technology had made the Atlantic cables redundant and both the Waterville and Valentia stations closed down. Many of their former telegraphists and workers emigrated and their departure was deeply felt in the region. The fate of the cables themselves also hung in the balance, with some proposing that the connections simply be cut and the cables sunk to the ocean floor. Joe C. Keating was one of those who recognised the financial and historic value of the cable.

Joe C. was born in 1931 on a forty-acre farm at Knockeens, just south of Caherciveen. As the youngest of nine, he watched all his older siblings emigrate to Manchester, Boston and New York, apart from two brothers who joined the Christian Brothers and are now enjoying retirement at Baldoyle on the north coast of County Dublin.

Any thoughts Joe C. might have had about emigration were overruled by his sense of duty to his mother, who was left a widow in 1941 when his father died of a brain tumour. 'I left school at fifteen to do the animals and mind my mother.'

As well as running the farm, Joe C.'s father, Maurice, and two of his brothers had operated a lucrative trade supplying Atlantic mackerel to the US army via the Billingsgate Fish Market in east London. When that business dried up at the close of the Second World War, Joe C.'s mother sent him to serve three years as a builder's apprentice in Caherciveen. The education did him the power of good and, together with a cousin, Joe C. Keating built houses, barns and sewage systems all across southwest Kerry, as well as unloading thousands of tons of rubble to both create and protect the highly rated Waterville Golf Links from the stormy ocean.

In 1965, Joe C. cruised out into Ballinskelligs Bay on board the 100-foot *Salvage Adventurer* and began hauling in the abandoned telegraph cables. He recovered over 300 miles of cable – some 3,000 tons – stripping it down into its individual components of raw rubber, electrolytic copper, lead, brass and steel. Joe C. was also a co-founder of the Cill Rialaig Arts Centre.

In his latter years, Joe C. has kept active. 'We had to use our wits to survive. The best university is the world itself. If you have a problem, you would have to resolve it. And we survived. We sharpened our brains. I take things easy now at eighty-two, but I still go out and I am still active and I associate with young people who keep me young. I don't think anyone should retire. You have to have some interest when you get up in the morning.'

Bronze Age ringforts, sandstone walls, Atlantic cables and conversation *as gaeilge*. There is no doubting that this part of Kerry is a world unto itself. It is also a world that is changing with each sunset. Just as the mighty cables that rolled along the Atlantic are now silent, so too the stories that Seán Ó Conaill and his friends relayed around the firesides of Ballinskelligs a hundred years ago are unlikely to be known by the children of the twenty-first century.

Opposite page: Tom Horgan.

Hannie Leahy

Annesgift, County Tipperary

Country Markets Secretary and Treasurer

Born 1919

'Everything is disposable nowadays,' observes Hannie Leahy. 'We were forever washing nappies in soap and water, putting them out on the line. Now you just put the nappy in the bin and get a new one!'

Hannie Leahy was born Hannah Crean in Fethard, County Tipperary, on 1 September 1919. Martin Crean, her father, was a gardener at Tullamaine Castle, a few miles northeast of Fethard, where the gardens were full of Victorian glasshouses for vines and peaches.

Martin was a man who dressed smart and sported a fine handlebar moustache. His wife, Ellen O'Meara, was the daughter of a neighbouring farmer and bore him a son, Willie, and two daughters, Hannie and Kitty.

Two of Martin's brothers and a sister emigrated to New Zealand and acquired land near Christchurch where they both raised large families. 'They never came home,' says Hannie. 'I suppose they hadn't the money to come back, and it took a long time to travel in those days. But their grandchildren come regularly, once a year nearly.'

In time, Hannie's only sister, Kitty, also emigrated to New Zealand with her Dublin-born husband, Brendan, who served as a prison officer in Wellington.

When Hannie was born, the War of Independence was in full flow. Assassinations, reprisals and the burning of entire towns as well as barracks and mansions caused widespread turmoil across the country. Tullamaine Castle, where she spent the first months of her life, was always under threat. One day, Martin was walking home with 'a big bough of wood' over his shoulder when a group of British soldiers swooped down upon him, thinking it was a rifle. He was fortunate not to be shot dead. By the close of 1920, Tullamaine Castle had been burned and looted.

After he left Tullamaine, Martin became gardener to the Hughes family at the Annesgift estate, close to the small farm where he had grown up, sheltered beneath the shadow of Slievenamon.

Hannie and her siblings enjoyed a relatively happy childhood with seemingly constant entertainment. 'There'd always be card playing and neighbours coming around for a chat, someone telling a few old yarns.'

Amongst the many photographs scattered around her home is one of the Moyglass senior hurling team who became South Tipperary champions in 1934. Hannie remembers almost every member of the team, not least her first cousin Johnjo O'Connor. 'There was lots of sport at that time. Hurling and football and camogie. I was never good at it, but I loved to watch.'

'When I was young, there was an awful lot of shops in Fethard,' she recalls. 'After I came out of mass, I would go to Cummins' for a penny-packet of sweets. And then another sweet shop started opposite the hotel. I think all the sweets came from the Geary's factory in Limerick.'

It wasn't just Geary's sweets that tickled the young Creans' appetite. 'We always had home-made bread during the week, but we used to love the weekend because my mother would buy two loaves of white shop bread for us!'

The children went to school in Coolmine, a half-mile walk across the fields from their home. 'It was short but it could be a terrible walk if the weather was against you.' The girls would arrive armed with kippeens, short thin sticks for the fire, while the boys would heave their way in with buckets of 'beautiful, lovely water' from the well.

One of her neighbours was her future husband, Jack Leahy. 'My husband, Lord have mercy on him, was born and reared in this house. I don't know when it was built, but I suppose it's the oldest house in the parish. When we were younger, we were always playing together. He was from a big family and his mother died when he was young. His father was wonderful and reared the whole family. Dan was his name and he was ninety-six when he died. He worked on the land in Annesgift, half-a-mile from here. Donal, my son, is the fourth generation to farm there, but I'm not sure if the fifth will be interested!'

Hannie left school at the age of sixteen. 'I loved school and I hated leaving,' she sighs. 'I still write letters, with paper and pens, nearly every day of the week. But, at that time, you had to pay for secondary education and I never had any chance of that.'

In 1935, she went to work in the Rectory in Fethard where Canon Patton, the local Protestant clergyman, operated a market garden. 'I was an under-secretary to Phyllis O'Connell, his secretary, doing all the invoicing and organising the dockets for all the plants to go off by rail. It was a lovely job and they were lovely people.'

Hannie remained with the Pattons until her marriage

to Jack Leahy in 1942. 'And then I had to go home and look after my children.' Alice Leahy, the oldest of the five children, is the co-founding director and guiding light of Trust, a voluntary organisation that looks after the homeless in Dublin. Then came Eileen and Donal, both married and living locally, followed by the twins Martin and Mary, born in 1956. 'My father was a twin and one of Eileen's boys had twins too, so it really does skip a generation,' she says.

During the 1940s, Jack and Hannie also befriended the Hughes family at Annesgift. 'Major and Mrs Hughes were wonderful people. The major was in the war. He was a good farmer. Mrs Hughes was a Cruickshank and married at nineteen but she had no children. She was a great woman and an amazing organiser. She worked for the National Council for the Blind and she was also involved in the Country Markets.'

In February 1947, both Hannie and Mrs Hughes took their seats amongst the founding members of Country Markets Ltd, establishing their first country market in Fethard.

'I am the only founding member of the Country Markets still alive,' she says with a reassuringly hearty chuckle. 'But we got the market going – and it's still going! In the very same place that we started in the town hall. I was secretary and treasurer for thirty-one years. We got all the smallholders to sell their eggs, vegetables and brown bread. Everything was home-produced, labelled, inspected, covered and properly priced. It ran every Friday morning from eight till eleven, and I think it has run every Friday ever since we started it, except for when Christmas falls on a Friday.'

Jack continued to work until he was struck down by a stroke in 1992 and died after a very short illness. In coming to terms with his passing, Hannie went to Lourdes four times. She was also much bolstered by their five children.

Her living room wall is papered in a style reminiscent of William Morris, with pictures of Pope John Paul II, St Martin, Jesus and the Sacred Heart running alongside photographic portraits of her family members, including a fantastic group shot of the entire Leahy clan from 1960 with the twins up front.

Hannie continues to be active, even if she does not travel as much as she used to. That said, she has now been to Lourdes six times and would like to go again. She still attends regional meetings of Country Markets Ltd, and the annual meetings in Dublin, where she might pop in for a quick browse around Clery's. She's been a pioneer since 1936, as well as an active member of the Irish Countrywomen's Association. Otherwise, it's all about crosswords, reading books, mass on Saturday evenings and a few rounds of twenty-five which she plays an impressive five nights a week during the autumn.

'I remember Mrs Hughes had a Phaeton, a two-seater pony cart, which she used to love taking off for a drive on the roads. There was very few cars at that time. Major Hughes was one of the first to have a car or a telephone. Annesgift 10 was his number. I hadn't a telephone until twenty years ago and if I wanted to make a call, I would go to the neighbours. Now everyone has a telephone in their pockets. It's all go-go now. Cars, here, there, everywhere. Rushing. There's no time for anything!'

James Ridge

Cashel, County Galway

Farmer and Seaweed Harvester

Born circa 1959

'I was working at a sugar factory in England, d'ya see? They had me on the spinners and that's how I grew the whiskers. Have you ever seen sixteen ton of white sugar on the floor? It's a sight for the eyes to behold. A man from Lettermullen once said to me that we should buy it all and bring it back for the poitín. When you're on the spinners, the steam rises up. The heat and the steam. It comes down a shoot and into the mixer. 'Tis very hot, boiling. And that's what makes the whiskers grow. 'Twas the same with the Wolfe Tones and Luke Kelly. It's the sugar that did it.'

When James Ridge tells you something like this, you are inclined to believe him. It's something about the way he sets his head to one side and focuses his intense eyes upon your own. Besides which, in terms of where his whiskers came from, boiling sugar fumes seem perfectly credible.

James was born and raised in this area where his parents, Martin and Kathleen Ridge, ran a bed and breakfast. Martin was 'a very tidy man, always out with the sweeping brush'. By day, he worked as a ganger for Galway County Council. He was also involved with the Local Defence Force during the 'Emergency' years – 'a bit of marching and practice' – while an uncle served in north Africa in the desert campaign.

James has always had one eye on army life. Several of his childhood friends joined the Irish army. The memories of some elicit a loud envious shudder from his lips, others warrant a long, approving growl. 'They were like the Wild Geese of long ago. They went out to Cyprus and the Congo and all over the world.'

James, a fluent Irish speaker, makes his living from small-scale fishing and farming, as well as gathering turf and harvesting seaweed. 'Ah sure, but I'm not too busy now,' he says, grimacing at the sky. 'I'm only working on a few bits of seaweed and there isn't much in the way of fish anywhere now.' His handsome visage has also secured him the occasional role as a model for the photographer Perry Ogden.

We said goodbye on the steps of his home where the television is tuned into the afternoon's horse racing. 'Anthony McCoy is in the saddle today,' he advises, with a particularly powerful wink. 'McCoy's a good jockey, as tough a man as you get. All bone and muscle. Pat Eddery was good too but, oh cripes, McCoy's good.'

Seamus McGrath

Killerig, County Carlow

Farmer and Actor

Born 1921

One of the more bizarre cases to come before the House of Lords in London in recent years was that of a Californian builder called Paul Fitzgerald who believes he is the rightful Duke of Leinster. Paul maintains that he is a grandson of Lord Desmond Fitzgerald, younger brother of the sixth duke, who was killed when a grenade accidentally detonated inside his tent on the Western Front in 1916. Paul believes that his grandfather was not killed in the First World War, but faked his death so that he could go undercover and lend his support to the cause of Irish Republicans. After the war, Lord Desmond apparently made his way to Canada and then settled in California where he died in 1967. If it all sounds highly unlikely, Paul Fitzgerald apparently spent over £1.3 million advancing his claim before the Lord Chancellor threw it out in 2009.

Seamus McGrath has had a long-standing interest in the Fitzgerald saga because his mother's family, the Nowlans, were tenants of the Duke of Leinster. They originally farmed land at Crophill, two miles east of Castledermot, but, in 1784, the second duke transferred Christopher Nowlan to another farm three miles southeast of Crophill at Knockpatrick, near Graney Cross.

In 1801, the same duke gave Christopher's son, William, a farm at Corballis. William Nowlan was Seamus McGrath's great-grandfather and it is thought that he fought for the rebels at the second Battle of Hacketstown in 1798. Seamus remembers going to an auction where his mother tried, in vain, to buy a pike used during that same bloody battle.

Perhaps inevitably, Seamus has a soft spot for 1798. While holding a well-thumbed biography of Michael Dwyer, the hero of Derrynamuck, he recounts the sad tale of a father and two sons caught making pikes in their forge at Graney Cross. 'They were taken to the top of a building and dumped out through the gable end windows with a rope around their necks,' he says with gravitas. When I ask whether the rebels would have fared any better if they had used bows and arrows instead of pikes, his eyes contract as another historical 'what if' attaches to his growing collection.

In the late nineteenth century, William Nowlan's grandchildren made a mass exodus to the USA. Of nine children, only one remained in Ireland, namely Peter Nowlan, the youngest child, who duly inherited both the farms at Knockpatrick and Corballis.

'My grandfather was a bit of a character,' says Seamus, who remembers Peter from his childhood. 'He was a genius in his own right and he made a colossal amount of money in the late 1920s. He foresaw the Depression and sold every animal he had, except the milking cow. A year and a half later, after the crash, he bought them all back for a fraction of the cost.'

In 1889, Peter Nowlan married Miss Margaret Whelan of Tinoran and they had a daughter, Mary. In 1920, she married Jim McGrath of Garyhunden, Tinryland, County Carlow. Mary was a cousin of Dr Robert Farnan, a well-known 'ladies doctor' and senator in the Oireachtas who is considered by many to have been Éamon de Valera's best friend. Dr Farnan lived at Bolton Abbey in Moone, County Kildare, and upon his death in 1965, he left the abbey and 300-acre farm to the Archdiocese of Dublin. The abbey is now run by the Cistercians and Seamus still attends mass there 'nearly every Sunday'.

When Seamus, the eldest of Jim and Mary's seven children, was born on 2 April 1921, the War of Independence was raging across Ireland. A week before his birth, the British army had issued an order urging 'every person within the townland of Carlow to remain within doors between the hours of nine o'clock, p.m. and five o'clock, a.m., unless provided with a permit in writing'. Seamus' father avoided the Troubles as best he could, hiding his single-barrel shotgun in the ruins of a Knights Templar monastery which still stands on the farm today.

One of Seamus' clearest memories from his childhood was a spring night in 1933 when the nearby mansion of Duckett's Grove burned down. It wasn't an unexpected event. 'A neighbour gave himself a lot of hardship putting it out but the following weekend it went up again so he let it on,' he explains, his eyebrows wavering.

He reserves greater condemnation for the 'scandalous behaviour' of the Land Commission when they demolished another nearby mansion, Russellstown Park, considered to have been one of the most elegant buildings in Ireland. 'It was a beautiful house, decorated to the last,' recalls Seamus, who sold many a box of apples to Russellstown's last owner, Colonel Steuart Phillpotts. The Land Commission attempted to sell the house to the Patrician Brothers but, when that plan fell through, they knocked the house down. 'They were vandals, that was all,' says Seamus. 'The house was in perfect condition.' Meanwhile, Colonel Phillpotts, an Anglo-Irish gentleman renowned for gifting fully laden Harrod's hampers to anyone he stayed with, moved to London and became a cab driver.

Seamus' school at Grange was only half a mile from home. He later attended secondary school in Tullow where he became an enthusiastic athlete, specialising in the 120-yard hurdles. His father had been an all-Ireland champion long jumper, and Seamus himself racked up some impressive medals, coming third in the 1953 All-Ireland and second in the Leinster championship twice.

Seamus left school aged eighteen and 'tricked about in insurance' for a while. He also indulged in his dramatic ambitions, working closely with the Tullow Macra na Feirme Drama Society for nearly fifteen years. In 1959, he starred as 'the son of the poor auld man' in a version of T.C. Murray's one-act rural drama *Spring*, which won an All-Ireland medal in Athlone. Critics hailed the play as 'very impressive' and 'deeply moving', while Seamus was applauded for his 'very sincere performance'.

When Jim McGrath passed away in 1961, Seamus and his brother took on the running of the 122-acre farm at Killerig. The following year, Seamus met Ita Nolan, a nurse fifteen years his junior, whom he dated for the next six years. In 1968, the forty-seven-year-old farmer married Ita and they settled on Mill Street in Tullow. Seamus' mother was still living at Killerig and, as he tactfully puts it, 'two women don't always live well in the one kitchen'. Seamus threw his all into the Tullow community, becoming one of the key organisers of the annual Tullow Agricultural Show.

Seamus' mother died shortly before Christmas 1971. Her bachelor brother, Christy Nowlan, had also passed away three months earlier, and so Seamus inherited the old Nowlan farm at Knockpatrick. It stood near an old graveyard and an ancient ringfort where St Patrick is said to have rested during his travels. Over the next thirty years, Seamus drove the six miles from Killerig to Knockpatrick every day, sometimes two or three times, to check all was in order with the farm.

Seamus has always been a great traveller. Early in his farming career, he realised that the best value livestock were not necessarily to be sourced at local fairs. As such, he frequently drove 240 kilometres north to the market in Enniskillen for his cattle. And when he decided to farm pure-bred Suffolk sheep, he took his truck across the Irish Sea and bought his flock from Scottish farmers in Balmoral and Kelso.

Seamus and Ita had three sons and a daughter. Ita passed away in 2003 and, since then, Seamus has lived with a trusty Labrador who knows exactly when and at whom to bark. The house where he was born and raised is now used as a cattle shed. It stands just opposite the old monastery and it is clear that Seamus feels a strong connection with this location. He runs his hands along walls cemented with ox-blood and points out the narrow slits through which defenders let loose their deadly arrows a thousand years ago. Elsewhere there are the two wells down which long-gone monks lowered buckets for fresh water. It is not so long since one of Seamus' brothers sighted a ghost, clad in a hooded cassock, heading up the Friarstown Road. 'One of the old stock,' smiles Seamus.

Roisin Folan

Inisheer, Aran Islands, County Galway

District Nurse and Midwife

Born 1929

In 1961, a thirty-two-year-old nurse from County Meath stepped off the ferry at Inisheer, the smallest and most easterly of the three Aran Islands in Galway Bay. Roisin Maguire had been assigned to work on the island for the next year. Over half a century later, she is still there.

Roisin was born in December 1929 on a farm at Annagh, near Oldcastle that her father, Brian Maguire, acquired from the Land Commission. Aided by his brothers, Brian built a farmhouse, employing a local carpenter called Bartle Monahan to undertake the joinery work. Brian was clearly so impressed with Bartle's work that he married his sister Mary Monahan in 1913.

Eight children followed, of whom Roisin was the youngest. Death stalked the family in the early 1930s. Roisin was still a baby when one of her small brothers died. The following year, her father Brian succumbed to pneumonia.

Roisin's eldest brother, Jim, took on the farm and helped Mary raise the younger children. Along with her other brothers, Jim hurled for the local team. Jim crafted a small hurley stick so Roisin could play with them by the side of the house.

By 1934, four-year-old Roisin was walking to school, a two-mile dash through the fields to an old church in Carpenterstown. 'We went barefoot from the first of May through until November. Splashing into all the puddles! Our feet got so hard that you'd barely notice the thorns. My mother would take them out and eventually I was able to take them out myself.'

In the winter, the Maguire children collected timber from the wood on their land which they brought to school and placed on one of the two fires that burned at either end of the old church. In the summer, they came with bottles of milk. 'And if it was a hot summer, the milk was probably gone sour by the time it was lunchtime.' Lunch itself was 'a couple of pieces of brown bread with butter and jam in it – if there wasn't jam in it, I wouldn't eat it. I think everybody hated school in those days,' she muses. 'The stick was used so frequently, it's not surprising. There was hardly a day when you didn't get beaten for something. Maybe you'd be writing with a pen and a big blob of ink would come down the pen, because you weren't used to it, and then you'd get a slap for blobbing.'

'I was very happy away from school,' she recalls. 'Even though we had very little and everyone was very poor. If you were big enough, you had to help out, weeding potatoes and turnips. I liked the haymaking but, later on, I had to help my sister Cáit tie the sheaves and that wasn't so nice! My brother Tom cut the wheat with a scythe. Lawrence made the sheaf and I would come in after and tie them up. You'd go home with your legs all scratched from the thorns and the briars and nettles or whatever was among it. My mother was always worrying about not having enough money to pay the rent. She worried because when she was young, she had heard of people being evicted. Tom would say, "Don't be silly, that's not going to happen." She always worried about money. But, apart from that, we children were happy enough. We made our own amusements. On long winter nights, we used to play Ludo or cards. Or a neighbour would come in and sit around the fire and they'd talk about things that happened in the past that they heard from their parents. I loved the ghost stories but then I'd be very scared and I'd have to go up to bed with a candle.'

From the age of fourteen, Roisin cycled to secondary school in Oldcastle where, homework aside, she enjoyed her time, emerging as a fluent Irish speaker. However, work opportunities were so scarce in Ireland that she had to emigrate.

In 1948, she crossed the Irish Sea and spent a year working at a convent school in Surrey where the Reverend Mother advised her to either become a teacher or train as a nurse. She opted for the latter, enrolling at the Royal Northern Hospital on Holloway Road in London.

By 1956, she was operating as a midwife in Tottenham for the Royal Northern, as well as Guy's and Alexandra Park. This was the era depicted in the popular BBC television series *Call the Midwife*. Roisin also found time to enjoy life in a city that was rapidly moving away from the horrors of the wartime Blitz into a new age of Queen Elizabeth II and reconstruction, *The Goon Show* and the Ealing comedies. 'Oh, we had a great old time when we were off-duty,' says she.

Nonetheless, she yearned for Ireland, especially after

visits home. 'Once I got to England I was okay, but it broke my heart every time I had to go back.'

She finally returned to Dublin in 1957 and worked at St Kevin's Hospital (now St James's) for the next two years. If she had a night off, she would head back to her family home in Meath, covering the fifty miles in an epic two-and-a-half-hour journey on a scooter. After a crash left her with a black eye, she set aside the bulk of a week's wages for a helmet.

In 1961, she embarked upon a six-month course as a district nurse with the Jubilee Nurses. This organisation was founded by a group of Irish Protestant ladies in the late nineteenth century to provide trained nurses who could care for patients in their own homes. Once she'd passed the test, they sent her to Inisheer.

It was supposed to be a short stay. And then she met Máirtín Folan on a visit to the twenty-six-acre farm where his elderly parents lived. 'We were married in Galway in February 1963. The guests came from all over – friends from Dublin, family from Meath and some of the islanders took the boat across.'

Eight children followed, which ensured Roisin was flat out keeping house for the next couple of decades. 'You get a routine going but between the cooking and the washboard, there wasn't a lot of time. You'd always be trying to catch the fine weather to dry the washing on the line.' The children are now scattered across the globe – Adelaide, Kentucky, Nottingham, Ennis.

The beautiful, low-lying Atlantic island of Inisheer is arguably best viewed from the air where you can see the intricate network of limestone walls, built by hardy men in centuries past. The walls were designed both to create fields from the broken ground and to provide shelter for cattle. The stone walls were also good at retaining heat, enabling the island to enjoy a micro-climate.

Roisin found island life difficult in the early days. 'Not having electricity was the worst,' she recalls. 'I had a little electric radio that I brought everywhere but I couldn't use it.' There was also a melancholy air because all the other young people 'kept on leaving' the island. Two of Máirtín's sisters moved to Boston while his brother settled in Hartford, Connecticut. Other islanders opted for California, Chicago and Springfield.

When we met Roisin, she took us for a walk to the ruins of a small tenth-century church near her home which was named for St Gobnait. Her island eyes rolled slowly over the contours of the hollowed-out stones outside the church and the dry-stone beehive huts where the early Christian monks lived.

And as she looked, she spoke. About her trip to see her son in Kentucky. About the evenings in the island pub where she would play fiddle and sing songs and converse with everybody else in Irish. And about the inevitable changes she has seen.

The biggest change has been social. Most islanders, be they indigenous or newly settled mainlanders, have a car to which they tend to retreat after mass, where a generation earlier people would have stayed around to chat. The nightlife has also changed, with musical evenings now a rarity although the island pubs still do a reasonable trade.

And as for the island's animals, while there used to be horses and goats everywhere, now there are hardly any. 'Everyone had a donkey,' she says. 'But there's only two left on the island now.'

As she heads towards her eighty-fourth year, Roisin keeps busy at the Áras Éanna Arts Centre where she gathers with other women from the island every Wednesday to crochet and knit. They are a versatile crew and occasionally they are to be found eyeballing a computer screen or rolling out their yoga mats.

'It's a long way from Tottenham,' says Roisin. 'But that *was* sixty years ago!'

Simon Murphy & Jimmy Murphy

Cattle and Sheep Farmers

Ballymurphy, County Carlow

Born 1929 & 1934

Sprawled high upon the Blackstairs Mountains, the Murphy brothers' farmstead is sheltered from the whistling winds by the rump of a grassy field, a maze of stone walls and a solitary row of Leyland cypress that seem to shiver incessantly.

Neither Sim nor his younger brother, Jimmy, know when the first Murphy came here – 'generations and generations' is their best guess. Murphys galore are recorded here in Knockymullgurry townland in the 1911 census, and when Sir Richard Griffith was making his valuations back in the 1840s, he recorded two Murphys 'of Knock', Andrew and Peter. Indeed, it's little surprise that the closest village is called Ballymurphy.

Ballymurphy is where the Murphys prayed. 'Oh, by God, we went to church every Sunday,' says Jimmy. 'And we prayed here at home too.' Given that their kitchen wall is bedecked with images of the Blessed Virgin, the Messiah, the pope and the Sacred Heart, that is not a surprise.

We watch Jimmy come down from the mountain where he has been up feeding his cattle. He may be eighty-six but Jimmy still rides up there every day, seated upon a well-trimmed work horse. The cattle feed is transported in a half-dozen white sacks, hung either side of the saddle, and bound with the same twine Jimmy uses as a belt.

Back in his kitchen, Jimmy spreads out his soot-black hands and urges us to take a seat. 'It's cold enough up there,' he says. 'Will you have a cup of tea?'

The tea is made with soft rain pumped from a mountain stream. We sit and drink a while.

The kitchen is but a stage upon which the 'generations' of Murphys past have likewise come down from the mountain, shaken off the cold and taken a seat. Sim has faint memories of an aged grandfather sitting in one of the chairs. When they were children, the room was full of uncles. One uncle sometimes disappeared to South Africa and would then come back again. 'He was a grand fellow,' says Jimmy. 'But then he went away and we never heard tell of him again.'

Their parents were Simon Murphy and Bridget Doyle, a farmer's daughter from Rahanna, three townlands away. Sim, born in 1923, was the fourth of eleven children, and their eldest son. Jimmy was one of the youngest siblings, which may be why he still goes through life as if he is as fit as a fish.

A century ago, there was a small community up here. The next-door house, now abandoned, was home to another Jimmy Murphy who lived with his wife, Johanna, and worked on the railway. 'You'd hear all the dogs bark in the early morning and you'd know Jimmy was away to work on the railways. The railways is a long ways off from here, out beyant Ballymurphy, but he walked there and back every day.'

Their school was in Inch, a three-mile trek through endless fields and ditches. 'Oh, by God, it was a long walk,' says Jimmy, as if he's still coming to terms with it. And it wasn't a particularly joyful place to arrive into. 'The teachers would hit you around the head a bit,' he says. 'I left school at fourteen. No more school after that. Straight to work. And there was plenty of work, all the time.'

Sim was already a seasoned farmhand by the time Jimmy left school. His father sometimes held him back

from school so that he could teach him how to farm. 'He was getting old, I suppose, and he wanted to learn me how to follow horses and that sort of thing.'

The Murphys never had a tractor. 'We didn't have the money,' explains Sim. 'And that's the way it was going here for a long time before machinery or anything come.' Instead of machines, they bred work horses. 'You'd want to be working two or three of them in the fields. You'd need at least two because one on its own is no good.'

A combination of man and horse built the dry-stone walls that surround the Murphys' farmstead, reminiscent of the Aran Islands. ''Twas shocking hardy men who built those walls,' says Jimmy. 'Lifting all those rocks up from the fields. How in the name of God did they do that?! And nothing only their hands to work with.'

Their cattle and sheep are scattered on chunks of grassland around the hills, although how many head and how many acres is anyone's guess.

In decades past, they would drive the cattle to the Kilkenny market, some thirty-five kilometres to the west. An annual highlight was bringing the sheep down to the fair in Borris on 15 August. 'That would be a grand day out,' says Sim. 'The whole town would be full of sheep, and people walking around with sheep. It might be the only time you'd see someone you knew in a whole year.'

It's astonishing that these two men still live this way in 2013. They are certainly of sturdy stock. They don't

drink, but not because they are pioneers. 'It's just that we didn't drink and that was that,' says Jimmy, before adding with a chuckle, 'apart from a cup of tea.' Nor do they smoke, although they 'were fond of that one time but, by God, we gave them up all the same'.

When pressed about how long he can keep the farm going, Jimmy concedes that 'it was all right when we were younger but it's nearly too much now'.

'I go up the mountain every day,' he says. 'A couple of hours or more. It takes that time to straighten it all out, start in the morning, go see this, see that, but sure I was always at it, do you know? It's not that there'd be money in it. You could be losing money at the same time, and you'd still be working, but you do.'

'I suppose for our age we're all right,' muses Sim. 'My father and his brother was the very same. But, to tell the truth, we got into form because we had sheep and cattle. We always used to buy them as stock for our own land, and we'd plant oats for the stock. That was the carry on the whole time. I tell you, it was a healthy kind of job on the land.'

Fortunately, they are not short of companionship. While we are there, they have visits from a niece, a great-nephew and a neighbour. Their farm also lies upon a popular walkway. 'They're all mad for the best of air,' marvels Jimmy. 'Sometimes you'd hear them walking past at twelve o'clock at night.'

Some of these hikers are apparently hunting for gold hidden by a renegade militiaman during the 1798 Rebellion. 'It was tried a lot of times but the gold didn't come yet,' chuckles Sim. 'It was never there I suppose. But some people are very eager for money. And do you know what I think of the country now? I think it's middling on and off. Would that be right?'

Noel Sheridan & Mick Cronin

Naas, County Kildare

Post Office Worker and Philatelist & Textile Manufacturer and Electrician

Born 1927 & 1930

'I heard someone on the radio say how the first Ryder Cup was presented nearly a century ago. Now, that made me sit up straight because it was actually first presented in the year that I was born. And that is not a century ago … but I suppose it's getting on for a hundred years so I must be too!'

So says Noel Sheridan, clerk, postman and sometime golfer.

'My father was born in about 1900,' says Noel. 'Like most people at the time, he had a sort of poverty-stricken time in his younger years. Education just wasn't available to poor people. And families were very big. There were seventeen in my father's family, so they had to fend for themselves from fairly early on. Trying to eke out a living was very tough. But they looked after one another and they were all good workers and they managed. The aim of most parents in the next generation was that their children should attend school for as long as possible and then get permanent, pensionable jobs. My two brothers, my sister and myself were always very grateful to our parents, who worked so hard for us. Their aim for me to have a permanent job was successful, as I spent fifty years and two months in the postal service.'

Noel was still at school when, aged fourteen, he secured work in the post office which he joined in 1941. He spent his first months delivering post to the householders of the surrounding district. That involved a hefty daily trek on his bicycle up and down the foothills of the Wicklow Mountains, out from Naas to Ballymore Eustace, around Hollywood and home again. 'You wouldn't think much of it when you're that age,' he assures me. 'It was the norm at the time for boys to cycle maybe ten or twelve miles away from their homes. Some of those who were at school with me in Naas cycled in from Hollywood and back again afterwards.'

Always good at maths, he was subsequently given an office instead of a bicycle and assigned clerical work. 'I went to Dublin where I spent short periods in the chief sorting offices on Amiens Street and Pearse Street. I was working on counters in offices all around the capital.'

Noel's father, Mickie Sheridan, and his uncle, Christy Sheridan, played Gaelic football for Kildare in 1921, defeating Laois, Carlow and Wexford, only to be felled by Dublin in a replay of the Leinster final.

Noel also liked to kick a ball about in his spare time. 'I was still living in Naas and I would take a bus home at weekends. Of course, there were always games on. I played hurling, soccer and Gaelic football but I was

Opposite page: Mick Cronin (left), Noel Sheridan (right).

63

just not up to the standard of my father. The sons of good sportsmen are never as good! That happens most of the time, with just a few exceptions. But I enjoyed it. I started playing soccer then for the local club in Naas, and for Eadestown and Dunlavin.'

Noel worked in the General Post Office in Dublin for twenty-five years, between the counters and the Philatelic Bureau. 'They had me looking after deposit accounts for stamp collectors. I also went on trips to philatelic exhibitions in London, Rome, Vienna and New York, where there'd be over a hundred countries represented and thousands of philatelists coming along. They were only short periods selling your wares, but it was great for me to see the world and we got many new customers from the trips.'

One of Noel's neighbours and former golf-playing friends is Mick Cronin, the eldest of thirteen children. He was eight years old when John Grayson Duckworth opened the Naas Cotton Mills in 1938. A group of weavers from Lancashire came to train the Naas locals in the skills of mechanised textile work.

Eight years later, Mick took his place amongst the workforce.

'Nearly everyone you'd meet of our vintage went through the cotton mills,' he says. 'The mills was a great employer. I'd say if you got everyone that went through, the number would run into thousands. There were lots of women there. Even when I was leaving, there were probably 250 people there.'

'We were weaving the cloth that they made the shirts from for the big shops in Dublin. The mills had a delivery man who would gather all the cloth up and take it away to Dublin. It didn't change an awful lot until the very latter years, when the weaving cloth from the looms and threads began to die a death. They were seemingly able to import a lot of woven cloth for a lot cheaper than we could make it. So they diverted us into making synthetic blankets instead.'

In 1959, two major aspects of daily life in Naas came to an end. The first was the railway, which closed to all traffic shortly after the Naas races in March. The second was at the Grand Canal, when the final barge cast off from its moorings.

Mick could sense that the end was also nigh for the Naas Cotton Mills and so, after eighteen years in the mills, the thirty-four-year-old decided it was time for a change of career.

Since the construction of the power station at Allenwood, Mick had watched the population of Naas escalate. New housing estates, new schools and new industries were springing up all around the town. And they all needed electricity.

'I went into the electrical business in 1960,' says he. 'I was part time at first and I stayed on at the mills until 1964. I had to start from scratch but it's better late than never. I did the courses with the TV places at Pye and Bush, and a bit of old self-study myself. And I spent about forty-five years at it then after that!'

He established his own company, Abbey Electrical Services, and was recruited for several of the biggest electrical jobs in Naas, including the Concrete Pipe Factory on Dublin Road and the Dennison Trailers manufacturing plant.

The Naas Cotton Mills, by then run by GenTex of Athlone, closed down in 1970, six years after he had finally left the company. 'The death knell had sounded for a long time,' says he. 'I did the right thing going out on my own.'

Michael Kane & Sean Whelan

Naas, County Kildare

Works Manager and Compositor & Printer

Born 1931 & 1927

'There's not many who'd do fifty years with the one company nowadays,' reckons Michael Kane. 'But I was fifty-one years in the *Leader*. That's a long stint, eh?'

Michael was fourteen years old when he joined the staff of the *Leinster Leader* in 1945. The weekly Kildare newspaper had been founded some sixty-five years earlier by Patrick Cahill, a Home Rule activist.

'I spent the first seven years serving my time as a compositor for a weekly wage of twelve shillings and sixpence. That was good money that time but it was a long week too. Forty-four hours, nine to six, Monday to Friday. Four hours of a Saturday morning. And two hours extra on Wednesday because the paper went to print the next day. This was in the hot metal days, before computerisation and all that. Newsprint was very scarce after the war. It all had to be imported from northern Europe. Apart from the weekly newspaper, there was a jobbing side of the business too, making all sorts of books. We did a lot of work for Maynooth College too, so we were always busy.'

George Kane, Michael's father, grew up in Swords, County Dublin. He often talked of how, as a boy, he said goodbye to his eldest brother John Patrick Kane when, for reasons unclear to the present-day Kanes, the boy was dispatched to County Leitrim to be raised by a grandmother. John Patrick subsequently emigrated to America where he ceased contact with Ireland and began to fade out of the Kane family annals.

Many years later, Michael and his daughter recruited an American genealogist who discovered that John Patrick had found work driving electric trains on the New York to New Haven railway line. Although he had died at the age of eighty-seven, they managed to track down his daughters.

'It was a proper Irish-American story of connections breaking and getting mended again,' says Michael. 'His daughters told us that, when they were young, all their Irish friends had uncles and aunts all over the place. But they never had any relatives until we found them!'

George Kane became a Civic Guard and was initially stationed in Bagenalstown, County Carlow. He later married a sister of Jack Higgins, the iconic Kildare footballer, with whom he settled at Highland View outside Naas.

Michael, the eldest of the four children, was works manager at the *Leinster Leader* by the time of his retirement in 1996. 'And since then it's been "One Day at a Time, Sweet Jesus", like Gloria sang,' he chuckles.

Amongst the forty or so employees at the *Leinster Leader* during this time was the printer Sean Whelan, who grew up one street away from the Kane family home. Sean's younger brother, Jim, was one of Michael's greatest friends. Jack Whelan, father of Sean and Jim, was a mechanic who played a key role in the breakout of some seventy Republican prisoners from the Rath internment camp at the Curragh during the War of Independence. He subsequently became a driver with the Free State army during and after the Civil War although, like so many of that generation, he never passed on the details of his experience to his children. 'Brother had been fighting agin brother so there wasn't much talk about it,' says Sean.

Many of Sean's aunts and uncles settled permanently in London. In 1947, Jack also moved to London where he remained for several years.

Sean also headed for the English capital in 1947 to gain some useful work experience. A passionate sportsman and lifelong pioneer, he was just sixteen years old when he started work at the *Leinster Leader* in 1943.

'I was sent to London by the *Leader* when I was twenty years old,' says Sean. 'I was on Feather Lane just off Fleet Street for three months, in a school where they taught me about mono-typesetters. I'll never forget the boat journey over to Liverpool. I was so sick that I lost my suitcase, which was full of eggs and chocolate. I found it eventually and I got to London okay. But the thing that got to me most about being away was that I missed the races at Punchestown. That was the first time I missed them. And the last.'

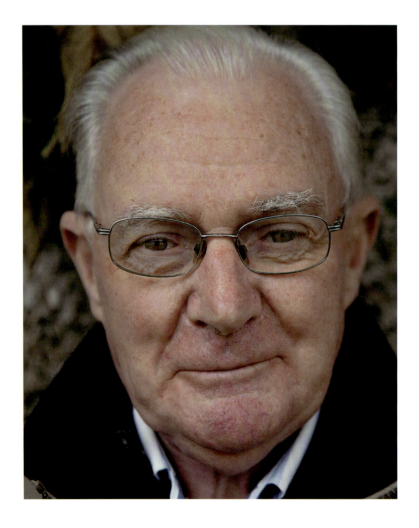

Eamonn King

Farravaun, Glann, Oughterard, County Galway

Cattle Farmer and Horse Breeder

Born 1937

'Would you believe that I cried when I stopped school? I loved it. I didn't want to leave. I thought it was the end for me.'

Rare words indeed for anyone educated in Ireland in the middle decades of the twentieth century. And yet, Eamonn is so genuine about his love for school that he soon launches into a ballad he learned from his teacher, Miss Leyden, about a strange encounter with the Blessed Virgin, Queen Victoria and Mary, Queen of Scots.

He doesn't sing the song. He recites it.

'I'd love to be able to sing, but I don't have a voice,' he claims, although I imagine that when he is alone upon a tractor, he belts it out like a baritone.

There were two teachers in his school in Glann and he liked them both. Nancy Leyden came from up the mountains and was not to be trifled with. 'Nancy would work the stick all right but she never gave me a tip with it.'

The other teacher was Mrs Manning, from Irishtown on the Galway–Mayo border, with whom Eamonn kept in touch until her death. 'She never once gave me a slap but she gave me a mug of tea every day.' And not just any old tea. It was Lipton's.

'Some of the lads used to call me the teacher's pet,' he admits, 'but that's beside the point. The teacher had the authority to let you out when help was needed in the springtime, following the horse and plough, spreading potatoes and seed. If you didn't know your catechism, you wouldn't be let out. I made sure I knew my notes and that gave me the freedom to get out.'

Eamonn was born on the farm where he has lived all his life. His father, Tommy King, was an adventurous soul. Born in 1881, Tommy was sixteen years old when he and his neighbour James Clancy ran away one Sunday morning. Tommy had stashed some money earned while working for the local landlord, Mr Hodgson of Currareevagh, while James had rustled up some money from the Clancy family trunk while they were all at mass.

The two boys took a train to Dublin and a ship to Scotland, and made their way to Glasgow where a man called Kelly put them up in a bug-infested shack. After a few months working long-shore in Glasgow and

Jarrow, Tommy saw a sign offering 'Passage to America'. He was to spend the next two decades in the USA where, joined by his younger brother, Pat, he worked in the copper mines of Butte in Montana, laboured on farms in North and South Dakota, and hunted for moose and elk amid the snow-swept wilds of Alaska.

In the late 1920s, the King brothers returned home with their hard-earned cash and bought a farm each. Tommy hadn't been in the country since the mid-1890s but he had met Éamon de Valera when the latter was on a fundraising trip to New York in 1920. Many years later, Eamonn and his sisters would find the, by then, worthless $100 and $50 bonds Tommy had bought to help bankroll the Irish government. He had never cashed them in.

Tragically, Eamonn's uncle Pat was fatally paralysed while throwing weights near Spiddal. 'He was to get married but he died sitting by the fire at the age of thirty-seven,' says Eamonn.

Tommy had lost touch with his other brothers, Michael and Coleman, who had become priests and settled in Idaho. In fact, Coleman was born after Tommy ran away so the two brothers had never even met. One year, Tommy returned to America and tracked down Coleman to a school in Kellogg, Idaho. He arrived unannounced to find his brother playing basketball. Coleman, known for his fiery temper, was berating a kid for having missing the basket. Coleman then had a shot at the hoop and also missed.

'Say, fellow, you ought to get yourself a basket,' said Tommy casually from the sidelines.

Coleman reeled upon the stranger. 'And you'd better take a walk down the highway or they'll be taking you out in a basket,' he warned.

'Whoah, now,' said Tommy. 'That's no way to talk to an old fellow who came three thousand miles to see you.'

They were destined to become great friends, and Coleman was a frequent visitor to the family farm at Oughterard during Eamonn's childhood.

In 1931, Tommy married Mary McDonagh and they had three children. Born in 1937, Eamonn was their only son. His two sisters have both passed way. One was a butter-maker who lived in Ballyshannon, County Donegal. The other was a nun who taught at the Convents of Mercy in Galway and Spiddal.

Eamonn may have been a teacher's favourite at school but, as a young teenager, he briefly flirted with his rebellious streak.

'When I made my confirmation, I took the pledge. But, God forgive me, I didn't keep it too long anyways. I tasted all kinds of drink – whiskey, brandy, rum, vodka, Sandeman's Port, nearly every drink that I came across. Anyone can open their mouth and let it fall down, but carrying it is another thing. And one time, when I was fifteen, I got mad drunk on poitín. The big man inside trying to get out. I drank nearly a bottle of it and I went to milk a cow and I fell and I had to be carried home. I was cracked, gone mad altogether. I came home to my father with a hangover next day and I think he thought I was going to be a proper renegade altogether. I was so mortified that I made a promise that I would never drink again. And I have not tasted alcohol now for sixty years.'

Having exorcised his drinking demons, he focused on work. Every morning, he would cycle along nine miles of sandy road to a bog beyond Oughterard where he gathered up turf for the council at sixteen shillings a week. He also served a short stint with the forestry department but he came back to help his father on the farm aged twenty-one, 'and I have been here ever since'.

Finding a wife was tricky enough. The parish priest opposed the very notion of courtship. When he heard Eamonn had been sitting with a girl, the priest accosted him. 'Only for I have respect for ye, I would give you a toe in the underpants,' said he.

Eamonn was unimpressed. 'How were you to get a wife if you weren't to meet and get to know them?'

In time, he met his beloved wife Peggy Connor, mother of their six children, at the dance hall in Oughterard.

The Kings' farm at Farravaun runs along the mist-shrouded southern shore of Lough Corrib. Lichen clings to every branch of the whitethorn, birch, hazel and oak that blossom from the dampened ditches. The rocks are covered in moss. This is one of the wettest parts of the west and it's a constant challenge to keep the farm sustainable.

'I'm all my life trying to improve the land, God help me', says Eamonn. 'All my life digging for gold, but I've not found it yet. This is all granite around here, and hungry for manure. And it's getting wetter.'

He points to a marshy field full of rushes, which he recalls ploughing a few years ago. Another field where he once grew oats has sunk and metamorphosed into a full-blown lake, complete with perch and roach that he suspects one of his fishing-mad sons may have something to do with.

On the higher ground, he farms cattle, including a particularly handsome and virile Charolais bull. As a boy, he drove the ancestors of these beasts across the mountains to the fairs at Maam Cross and Spiddal. It was an arduous trek and 'the cattle would lie down for two days afterwards, never mind me'. Once or twice, he took them straight into the Fair Green at the heart of Galway city.

He also still breeds a few draught horses, which he rode in his younger years, although he has moved away from the Connemara ponies he once raced at the Oughterard Races.

Towards the end of our visit, Eamonn shows us the mossy ruins of a house built in a sheltered hollow beside one of his fields. Long years ago, he met a man who had once visited the old woman who lived here. She shared the house with a cow, which she kept tied behind the door. During the man's visit, the cow had a call of nature. Dreadfully embarrassed, the woman belted the cow and then addressed the startled creature, 'Sorry to hit you, but you've no manners before a stranger.'

'Poor thing, God love her,' sighs Eamonn. 'Weren't they tough times?'

Bridget Aspell

Yellowbog, Kilcullen, County Kildare

Shop Assistant and Housewife

Born 1910

Catherine's Cross is where it all happened. 'That said,' counsels Terry Lawler, 'Mammy is the only one I ever heard calling it Catherine's Cross.' Bridget Aspell, her 102-year-old mother, explains that the crossroads was named for a woman called Catherine who lived in the house beside it.

Bridget used to visit Catherine's Cross nearly every weekend back when the world was eighty years younger than it is today. Down by the cross, she would find the familiar faces, all gathered for the dance.

The idea of a crossroads dance sounds like make-believe to our twenty-first-century ears, but Bridget remembers those halcyon evenings with absolute certainty.

'There were dances all over Ireland at that time,' she says. 'There was another near us at Halverstown Cross, but we always went to the one at Catherine's Cross. All my uncles played accordion and sometimes they'd be out there too.'

Bridget's uncles were the Cummins brothers – Brian, Paddy, Myles and Bill. All four worked as labourers on the short-grass farms of County Kildare, although Myles, for one, served his time during the War of Independence. 'He was given medals by the IRA,' she says. 'That was years ago, when being in the IRA was a badge of honour.'

Along with Bridget's mother, Margaret, the Cummins boys were the children of Jim and Mary Cummins of Yellowbog, near Kilcullen, County Kildare. The house where they were raised stood just off the old Carlow Road, close to both Catherine's Cross and a pub called Brennan's which still runs today.

Born in Naas in 1890, Margaret had found work as a housemaid with one of the gentry families of Kildare during her mid-teens. In 1910, she gave birth to a daughter, Bridget. The father's name is unknown. This was dangerous terrain for many women of that era who, for the sin of motherhood, all too often found themselves virtually imprisoned in a workhouse or a Magdalen Laundry.

Fortunately, Margaret's mother offered to raise the baby while the younger woman continued to work as a house servant.

Until she was ten years old, Bridget's grandmother was the most important woman in her life. 'My granny could do everything,' she marvels. 'She knitted and sewed; she was great at embroidery. She made it all with her hands. I remember the collars she made for the gentry. Sometimes, she would call at their houses with the collars and sell them. But sewing wasn't a skill I inherited. It's the last thing I can do!'

On the eve of the First World War, Bridget's mother married Peter McGlynn and settled at Twomilehouse, south of Naas. The McGlynns had seven children whom Bridget absolutely regards as her siblings – Peter, Billy, Rita, Jimmy, Mary, Mags and Lizzy. The latter two died as infants while the rest have all since passed, bar Mary.

Following the death of Bridget's grandmother in 1920, her mother's sister Maryanne took on the role of rearing the young girl. 'They were tough times,' recalls Bridget. 'Things were very scarce. Maryanne would go to early mass and when she came home, her neighbour would borrow her coat and shoes to go to the next mass.' Many decades later, Maryanne would come to live with Bridget for the last seven years of her life, dying at the age of ninety-seven.

Bridget maintains that her childhood at Yellowbog was a happy one, even if there were not many others living in the area. In the wintertime, they would gather to watch the hounds and horsemen of the Kildare Hunt set off through the gorse and marshlands in pursuit of the fox.

During term time, she would meet up with the Dixon girls, good friends who lived nearby, and they would all walk the three miles from Yellowbog to their school in Kilcullen. This coincided with the War of Independence and Bridget recalls a morning when the notorious Black and Tans drove into the town. 'We all ran down from the school to the square to see them with their guns. That's the first time I seen the Tans.'

Fortunately, while a number of houses were burned during the ensuing conflict, the Cummins home escaped unscathed.

From school, she went to work at Orford's pub in Kilcullen, now known as The Spout. Her role was to keep the shop swept and polished before, during and after it opened for business. However, she was much happier when the Orfords, or the Brophys, a farming family she also worked with, gave her jobs to do outside.

'I worked in fields all my life. I loved the outside work – picking potatoes, thinning and snagging turnips. You'd pull them out of the ground, snag the top off and lay them all in a row on the ground. Ah, they were different times to now. People were much more homely then. If you wanted anything on the run, people would give it to you. But then people got more uppity and they don't like to depend on other people. They want to be independent, I suppose.'

One Saturday evening, Bridget was making her way out of the chapel when a man at the corner stood out from the wall and started talking to her. 'And that's how I met my husband,' she laughs.

Paddy Aspell had been working as a gardener at Knocknagarm on the edge of the Curragh since he was fourteen. After twenty-three years there, he was to spend over forty years as gardener for the jockey T.P. Byrne in Lumville.

The Aspells lived in Sunnyhill, two miles out of Kilcullen, where they raised eleven children, one of whom died young. Ever the land girl, Bridget frequently walked across the fields from Sunnyhill to Calverstown, to pick potatoes for the O'Connors of The Orchard. 'And then I'd go home and get the dinner for the rest of them,' says she with a wry smile. 'I done two days work in one.'

Paddy and Bridget enjoyed sixty-two years of marriage before a lifetime of chain-smoking got the better of him in 1991.

Bridget now lives with a daughter on the edge of Kilcullen, surrounded by her family. On the kitchen dresser of her present home stands a fine photograph of herself at Burtown Gardens near Athy in the summer of 2012. She is seated on an elaborate swing designed by Sasha Sykes beneath the caption 'Definitely the Oldest Swinger in Town'.

She enjoys life with the aid of a midday whiskey and a weekly trip to have her hair done by her granddaughter, Hazel Lawler, in Narraghmore. A great-niece, Josephine Archbold, brings communion up to her every week. Bridget graced the front page of the *Leinster Leader* when she did the honours as Grand Marshall of the 2013 St Patrick's Day Parade in Kilcullen.

She also still enjoys her musical outings. 'I love music,' she says. 'It's the céilí for me. I am sorry I didn't learn to play an instrument. My granny was a good singer. She used to sing ballads and old-time songs at weddings. But I don't sing myself. If I started, everyone would leave the place. But I could stay up all night listening to it.'

Patsy Dalton

Athea, County Limerick

Denim Maker, Turf Cutter and Chef

Born 1950

They say the sleán is as scarce as the corncrake in west Limerick these days. But should you chance to be in the vicinity of Athea during the springtime, you might yet espy a handful of men who still head out to the bogs to harvest the turf with their brawny shoulders and razor-sharp sleáns. And if one of them is sporting a moustache, a pipe and a denim flap cap, you're almost certainly looking at Patsy Dalton.

Patsy's skill at the ancient art of turf-cutting is genetic. His late father was one of the most noted bogmen in the county. Patsy also possesses some of the warrior spirit of his ancestor Sir Walter D'Alton, a Norman horseman who came to Ireland with Strongbow in the twelfth century. During the religious upheavals of the seventeenth century, a Catholic branch of the family was pushed south into the barren bogs of west Limerick.

Patsy's grandfather, Michael 'Cooper' Dalton, hailed from Athea and descended from this Catholic branch. He was an accomplished cooper who specialised in making 'mate barrels' for storing bacon following the killing of a pig, as well as churns for making butter and small barrels, called firkins, for transporting the butter to the Cork Butter Market.

Patsy's late father, Mick, one of eight children, was born in Glenbawn in 1913 and worked as a block-layer for the building contractor Jimmy Reidy. Mick was also an exemplary turf cutter and Patsy recalls how his father's stride became utterly reinvigorated every March as the turf-cutting season approached. He had a bank on the Blane Bog between Athea and Glin and indeed this is the very same bank that Patsy cuts today. The road leading into the bog was constructed in 1942, providing considerable local employment. As the war in Burma was dominating newspaper headlines at the time, the locals christened it 'The Burma Road'. Blane Bog itself is sometimes called 'The Burma' and is the subject of a popular poem by Thomas J. O'Donoghue of Drumrisk.

Like his father, Patsy keeps his swathe of bog in good order, the sides level, the base water-free. He works with a sleán to create even, rectangular sods of turf which he spreads alongside the bank. He then transfers the sods to a timber bog barrow which he wheels out to the road. When he started, the bogs were black with people harvesting throughout the spring months. There were at least three men – and maybe five or six – on every bank. At tea breaks, stories, yarns and fibs would drift through the air. One or two of the men might sing. Tim Joe Riordan, one of Patsy's closest friends, could deliver a powerful rendition of Jack Riordan's 'Lovely

Athea', a ballad lamenting the execution of local hero Con Colbert after the Easter Rising of 1916. Otherwise, the predominant sound was the sleáns slicing through the turf, with maybe a lark or a swallow or a cuckoo whistling in the distance.

Patsy, one of three children, was born at the Green Lawn Hospital in Listowel on a snowy December morning in 1950. He grew up in the same low-lying whitewashed roadside cottage where he lives today. He reckons the building has been there for over two hundred years. In his childhood, part of the house was occupied by a country shop. Mrs Casey, who ran the shop, sold tea, sugar, cigarettes, bread and paraffin oil but closed it down when the supermarket opened in Athea in 1969. Families from throughout the district brought their eggs to Mrs Casey's shop from where they would be collected by lorry and taken off to places like O'Neill's bakery in Abbeyfeale.

Like many families, the Daltons kept their own pigs, slaughtering one in the autumn and another in the

spring. 'It takes three months to fatten a pig,' Patsy advises. 'You'd give him all the small potatoes and the waste so it wouldn't cost you anything to feed him.' On the appointed day, the pig would be killed with a mallet and hung up on a ladder. Once its brains and innards were removed, the pig was cut into pieces on the kitchen table, salted with a knife and placed in a barrel of water for the season ahead. 'The nicest pig of all is a young sow after the first litter,' says Patsy. 'That gives you the loveliest streaky bacon.' His mother also made a spicy black pudding, the memory of which still makes Patsy's mouth water.

Local tradition dictated that on the day the pig was killed, the children of the family would go around to the neighbours, offering up the best parts. 'You started with the two hams and they were nearly gone by the time you got home,' says Patsy. 'And you gave away all the best of the lean meat too. We were feeding maybe sixteen neighbours at that time.' However, as everyone had pigs which they reared and slaughtered, the good meat came full circle when the neighbours' children came a-calling.

In those days, wild goose was a particularly popular specialty. When geese were flying low, the people would lure them into V-shaped pits, laden with wheat, sunk into their small fields. Once in the trap, the goose could not escape and so, as Patsy says, 'you'd have goose for dinner that night which made a nice change from the bacon'.

Perhaps it was the spiced black pudding and the wild geese that stirred Patsy's culinary instincts. After he left school in Ballyguiltenane, which he hated, he made his way to Copsewood College, a secondary school outside the village of Pallaskenry, County Limerick, run by the Salesians of Don Bosco. The school includes an agricultural college where Patsy studied from 1970 until 1979. For the last five years, he also worked as a cook in the college kitchens, providing food for nearly two hundred and seventy students. The school slaughtered their own meat until 1973 when a new European law decreed that a person had to be certified to slaughter animals. Henceforth, a butcher was recruited for the slaughter.

In 1979, Patsy bade the Salesians adieu and made his way to Tralee, County Kerry, where he worked with Burlington Industries, an American company that specialised in the manufacture of a new washable polyester and wool blend called Burlana. Shortly after his arrival, the company began expanding into denim apparel fabrics and, as the age of Levi 501s and Wranglers began to dawn across the Western world, so Patsy began making denim rolls 'a mile in length' which they packed into containers and sent back across the Atlantic. His denim cap is something of a nod to that era.

In 1982, Patsy left Burlington to help complete the billion-dollar Aughinish Alumina refinery on Aughinish Island, which lies in the River Shannon. Completed the following year, this was the largest construction project in Europe at the time, employing up to 6,500 workers. It is said the money generated for the region put a washing machine in every house in west Limerick. 'It was a big job but great money,' agrees Patsy.

He is uneasy about the refinery. With millions of tons of red sludge being pooled in a series of containment tanks alongside the Shannon, he can't help but think of the disaster that struck the River Danube when the aluminium refinery in Hungary burst in 2010. Bear in mind that Aughinish used to be a peninsula until it was torn away from the Irish mainland in 1755 when a freak earthquake in Portugal sent a tsunami crashing up the Shannon.

When he finished at Aughinish, Patsy went to work in the bogs, harvesting the peat with his sleán from early morning until the sun went down. 'We were always looking for gold but we never feckin' found any,' he laughs. 'Someone got a lump of bog butter one time. It's meant to have been buried there for a thousand years and still edible but I wouldn't try it in an omelette.'

Bridget O'Malley & Penny O'Malley

Aillebrack, County Galway

Housewives

Born 1932 & 1937

Over six billion human beings now own a phone, mobile or cell – call it what you will. If you want to speak to almost anybody on the planet, all you need are the right digits and you could feasibly be having an ear-to-ear chinwag in less than 30 seconds.

'Twas not ever thus. When Penny and Bridget O'Malley were youngsters, making a phone call was a long and complicated procedure. If they were better at it than most, that is because their brother, Michael King, looked after the only phone in the neighbourhood. It stood in the post office which he ran at Drimmeen, on the westernmost tip of Connemara's Errislannan Peninsula.

The Errislannan post office had been the preserve of the O'Malley family since the nineteenth century when Bridget Coyne, grandmother of Penny and Bridget, ruled the roost. Born on the eve of the Great Famine in 1844, she married Tom King, scion of a family who have been ensconced on the peninsula since time began. Mrs King always dressed in a long black skirt that matched her jet black hair, with a white shawl draped over her shoulders.

In 1926, two years before Mrs King's death, her eldest son, Donald, took on the post office. In Donald's day, all the post was delivered by a man on a bicycle, his big, black cape fluttering over his handlebars and front basket to try and stop the driving Irish rains soaking into the packages and letters. The service was inevitably much slower at Christmas time and the poor man would still be pedalling around the pothole-plenty Connemara roads long into the night. If the weather proved too severe, he would rest up at the Kings' house until the break of dawn. 'They put in some hard days,' says Penny. 'But I tell you it didn't do them any harm; they all lived to a good old age!'

Postmen and postmistresses alike must have wondered at the future possibilities of communications when, in June 1919, Captain Alcock and Lieutenant Brown completed the first non-stop trans-Atlantic flight from America to Europe. Their plane crash-landed on the spongy blanket bog of Derrygimla, close to the school in Ballinaboy where the O'Malley sisters were later educated. The fearless duo flew 1,800 miles across the ocean in an open-cockpit Vimy. Their extraordinary adventure dominated the banter around every kitchen table in Connemara for many months after the event.

Opposite page: Bridget O'Malley.

One of the Kings' neighbours, Pateen Conneely, was working in the Marconi radio station beside the bog where the plane landed. As his work colleagues ran out to see whether the pilots had survived, Alcock stood up from his seat, removed his goggles and announced, 'We are Alcock and Brown. Yesterday we were in America.'

In 1925, six years after Alcock and Brown's landing, Donald King's brother, Stephen, married Penelope O'Malley, the daughter of a farmer from Rosmuc near Carna, County Galway. Six children followed, two sons and four daughters, including Penny and Bridget.

The girls enjoyed a quiet and contented childhood. They went to school in Ballinaboy, a three-mile walk from their home. The building was later demolished, but the pillars still remain. Their world was a small one. Bridget did not visit Dublin until she was eighteen. They may have cycled all around their native peninsula but generally it was a slow and steady pace of life. 'People used to be gathered around talking at crossroads and by walls and things. Today people don't have time to talk because everyone is rushing on to the next thing!'

During the Second World War, Ireland's neutral government established a series of lookout stations across Ireland, complete with telephones which operators could use to inform the authorities that German, or perhaps British, bombers were looming overhead. One such station was built upon Doon Hill, close to where the O'Malley sisters live today. When these stations were decommissioned after the war, the telephone from Doon Hill was dispatched to the sub-post office on Errislannan where Bridget and Penny's eldest brother Michael had now succeeded as postmaster.

Bridget and Penny laugh as they recall the kerfuffle of making a phone call in those times, dialling the number over and over again as you sought to make contact with the telephone exchange in Clifden, and then waiting an age while they attempted to connect you to the person you actually wanted to speak with. Each call had to be logged in a book, complete with its time and length. As the postmistress was invariably listening in to the call, everyone had to be excessively polite to one another. 'There was no gossip talked down the line,' laughs Bridget.

In September 1952, Bridget King married Pádraig O'Malley of Aillebrack, a muscular fisherman who spent his days at sea in a twenty-eight-foot fishing boat, hauling up baskets of lobster and crayfish, or reeling in salmon from the pier by his home. He sold his catch from the pier at Bunowen, to which buyers came from all over Galway and Clare. When French ships moored off Aillebrack, the lobsters that Pádraig caught sometimes went all the way to the fine restaurants of Paris. Shellfish and salmon formed a major part of Bridget's daily diet, and she confesses she got utterly bored of both. She and Pádraig had eleven children, ten of whom are still alive and scattered between Chicago, Dublin, Galway and the Aran Islands.

On 19 March 1955, Bridget's younger sister Penny waved goodbye to Ireland from the decks of RMS *Saxonia*, an ocean liner that set out from Cobh and docked in New York six days later. 'Everyone on the boat was Irish and we were all going to America to start a new life. There was great excitement. A lot of people from south Connemara went to Chicago, and I had cousins in Cleveland also. Others were headed for New York and Boston. But the voyage was lovely, no gales or anything, and there was so much to do. Every morning, they put a programme under your door telling you about all the entertainments they had planned for the day, the films and dances and things. It was like a holiday cruise really!'

On reaching America, Penny headed west to Pittsburgh where one of her mother's brothers was working in the steel mills. She spent the next five years in the city, working as a housekeeper with a well-to-do family called Evans. Every summer, the family headed six hundred miles west to Cape Cod for their holidays. Penny travelled with them and then went to visit her own relations in Boston and New York.

In 1960, she received word that her mother was seriously unwell back in Connemara, so she packed her bags, thanked the Evans family and flew home in time to be by her mother's bedside when she passed away.

Opposite page: Penny O'Malley.

'I'm glad I went to America,' she says, 'but I'm also glad I came back because this is where my family were.'

In 1962, Penny married Jimmy O'Malley, younger brother of Bridget's husband Pádraig. Jimmy was the first of his family to become a blacksmith, learning his trade at the Technical College in Ballinasloe. He started off shoeing workhorses but quickly realised that tractors were overtaking horses as the beast of choice for most farmers. 'Horses were actually a lot harder work than tractors,' says Penny. 'You had to run out in the morning to catch them, where you could just get up on a tractor and turn the key! And a tractor could do in an hour what might take a horse a day.'

Jimmy's welding skills became ever more elaborate and, during the mid-1950s, he won several competitions, including a prize at Dublin's An Tóstal festival for a hand-forged candlestick holder he had designed. His skill as a farrier also brought him work with both racehorse owners and movie producers, and his handiwork can be seen in films such as *Into the West* and *Three Wishes for Jamie*. He also taught metalwork on the Aran Islands.

Penny and Jimmy had five children, two sons and three daughters, before his premature death in 1991. Their eldest son, Thomas, tried to keep the forge going but had to abandon it in 2004 when the microscopic fumes from the welder began to infect his lungs, a pertinent reminder of just how poisonous blacksmithery can be. Thomas has since framed a wonderful array of the horseshoes his father designed, all branded with the 'James O'Malley' stamp. It's easy to think horseshoes are a 'one size fits all' procedure but Jimmy's collection shows the contrary to be true as he created tailor-made shoes to counter the various diseases that can afflict a horse's hoof. The samples displayed carry names such as corn, French rocker, single dub toe, double dub toe, normal fore, full bar and three-quarter bar.

The landscape around Aillebrack was smothered in holiday homes during the Celtic Tiger years, particularly with the opening of the nearby Connemara Golf Club. Today, holiday homes easily outnumber those that are occupied all year round. 'But the actual population has not changed that much,' says Penny. 'A lot of people went to the States and did well in construction and things. Then they came back and built some fine houses. I suppose families are smaller now, but more people have stayed. In the last twenty years, there was hardly any emigration. That has changed again now unfortunately. If there's no work, the young people will go away again.'

Denis Lee

Inistioge, County Kilkenny

Blacksmith, Sheep Shearer, Hackney Driver and Drummer

1923–2012

When Denis Lee's daughter, Gemma, ushers us into his home on Inistioge's Mill Road, she warns us that the eighty-seven-year-old might be 'a little tired today'. Tired he may have been, but Denis was as alert and erudite as any man I've ever met. By the time we left one hour later, I calculated that he had spoken in excess of eight thousand words, allowing for an average speed of one hundred and forty words per minute.

I think he lived his whole life at that pace. He was an extraordinarily busy man. As such, it did not surprise me when I heard that the guard of honour at his funeral was formed from the combined forces of the Rower and Inistioge GAA Club, the Inistioge Sheep Shearers, the Fine Gael party and the Nore Vale Harriers. With music by the Graiguenamanagh Brass Band and John Burke, it was a very fitting farewell.

Denis Shelly Lee was born on 18 September 1923 in the beautiful south Kilkenny village of Inistioge, which sits on the River Nore. The family had been blacksmiths in the area for innumerable generations. Their forge stood at the bottom of the village square.

His father, John, one of eleven children, took an active role in the War of Independence as a young man. The forge narrowly escaped discovery as the source for the metal spikes used to puncture the tyres of the Crossley Tender trucks driven by the Black and Tans. The Tans were stationed at Woodstock House, a splendid mansion above the town, subsequently burned during the Civil War. One of John's brothers was incarcerated on Spike Island and later emigrated to New York.

Denis, the third of five children, went to work in the forge from an early age, helping his father bend the red-hot cart wheels. 'I started as soon as I was able to blow the bellows,' he said. 'I left school when I was about thirteen and I was tipping away in the forge from then on.'

There were long periods when his father did not require any assistance in the forge. Eager to keep himself occupied, young Denis seized the opportunity to help his neighbours. When he wasn't milking cows in Inistioge – and there were six families in the village with cows at that time – he was helping out on a cousin's farm, bringing in hay, taking out the chaff, riding up on a horse and cart. He also befriended Paddy Delahunty, a sheep farmer who lived on the nearby Hatchery Lane.

'I was only a baby when I started to follow after Paddy. I'd help him out with the sheep. I learned every class of a trick that could be done with a sheep. Skinning and butchering. Cutting off lambs' tails in the spring time. Castrating them with a penknife. Killing the lambs for Easter. Herding them to the fairs in Graiguenamanagh and Thomastown. And I sheared sheep in five different counties.'

He sheared his first sheep at the age of nine and was to become one of the most skilled sheep shearers in the southeast. 'I did sixty-nine one day with a shears. It was sixpence a piece that time, thirty-five shillings, and I went to the Gowran Races the next day.'

By the late 1940s, with the assistance of a Fordson Major tractor, he was bailing straw throughout the region, including 'all the wheaten straw they put under the hunting horses' at Mount Juliet, the headquarters of the Kilkenny Hunt. 'We'd cut corn with a binder, make the stooks and thresh with all the neighbours.' In 1948, his cousin Andy Gorey bought a thresher set. 'And I gave twenty years after that, threshing for all the farmers around, but then the combine came in and that finished the thresher set.'

In 1950, Denis purchased a Fiat for £50 and set himself up as a hackney driver, primarily escorting people to Kilkenny hospital, to funerals and to mass. He even drove children to school in it. 'No one had a car back then. I used to bring people to eight o'clock mass every Sunday morning. I'd make three runs then of a Christmas morning. One auld lad always had a big naggin of whiskey with him.'

Sometimes, he drove people to catch the ferry to England from Rosslare. 'I never left Ireland myself,' he said. 'I wouldn't like to be out in the middle of the sea like that. I like to be my own man.'

He did once accept an offer from a friend to step into a fishing cot which was berthed on the shore of the Nore. 'I didn't think he had any drink on him, you see. "Come on!" he said. "And we'll have a little spin down the river." So in I got and he never stopped until we got to New Ross. It was the month of September, freezing. When we got to Ross, in we went to the pub for a pint, and we stayed a while, but I got home anyway because I had to bring a load up for the All-Ireland in Croke Park next morning. I wasn't worth tuppence, as the fellow says, but it was good craic while it lasted.'

The list of what Denis did goes on. He was a reserve postman. He dabbled in undertaking. And like his father and grandfather before him, he was a blacksmith. When Eddie Macken's show-jumper Boomerang lost a shoe at the Inistioge Horse Show in June 1979, nobody had any doubt about who should be summoned in to re-shoe the legendary horse. The photograph of Denis with Boomerang was amongst his proudest possessions.

As the years went by, his car got bigger. By the 1970s, he was frequently escorting groups of hurling fans up to Croke Park. 'Everyone would be singing and shouting and fighting and arguing over the hurling the whole way up and down.' On the journey back, they would partake of refreshments in a variety of establishments in Leinster, including the Workingman's Club in Carlow.

Denis always enjoyed a good time. He was a familiar face at both horse and greyhound race meetings all over Ireland. His own greyhounds won numerous races along the way. With his big bass drum, he was also a musical icon across south Kilkenny. He was a ten-year-old boy when he joined St Colmcille's Brass Band in Inistioge, initially playing tenor horn and cymbals, alongside his father on the big drum and his brother, Jim, on the baritone horn. When his father retired, Denis took over his big drum and, together with Jim, joined the Graiguenamanagh Brass Band. He had lost count of the number of times he played the 'Dead March' at funerals, but reckoned he spent twenty consecutive St Patrick's Days marching with the band through the streets of Kilkenny. Each year, without fail, he gathered and supplied shamrock for every band member. And when the drinks were on later in the evening, he would tip back his head and hammer out the verses of 'Boolavogue' or 'The Rose of Mooncoin'.

Denis Lee was laid to rest alongside his late wife, Breid, in Cappagh cemetery, just north of Inistioge, on 11 April 2012. They are survived by their three daughters, Mairead, Maura and Gemma.

Pat Fitzpatrick

Drumloona, Carrigallen, County Leitrim

Farmer and Actor

Born 1931

'But if you had joined the American army in the late 1950s, you'd have had to go to Vietnam,' says I.

'I know!' replies Pat, drawing out the word 'know' like he's registered this point a million times. 'And I would have loved that. I would love to have gone to Vietnam.'

Instead of serving his time with the Marines, Pat had to make do with a stint in the Local Defence Force in County Leitrim. But even that experience convinced him of the benefits of military life.

'I think the army is the best place any young lad ever went. You have to do what you're told. You learn to wash and clean yourself every morning, and make your bed. You're trained in the best of manners. You could train to be a mechanic, a shoemaker, a cook, whatever it is, they train you. The army never says, "We'll try this." They say, "We'll do it."'

Pat never got to America. His mother, whose brother had vanished into Ohio as a young man, was hostile to any form of emigration.

'My mother – God be good to her, I hope she is in heaven – she had a horror of America and thought I would lose my religion. "Rotten, dirty England," she'd say. And America was worse. This was drilled into me every day and I believed it until I was about twenty-eight. I thought that if you went away to America you'd be in the dump, rotting. She got over the point well. She kept me at home anyway. A lot went to America to earn a few pound and they were supposed to bring it home, but then they started to do well and they forgot to come home. So I didn't know any better. But then I used to see people who came home from England and America, like Johnny Doolin and Father Kevin Rourke. And to me they were like models. They told me it wasn't so bad. But I had lost the race by then and gotten too old.'

Pat is by no means embittered about having to stay at home and his speech is peppered with humour. It's simply that his mother was a force to be reckoned with. She was a farmer's daughter from Curraghboy. Pat has hazy memories of her father trotting past the house with a horse and cart when he was a baby. It's the same farmhouse where he lives today, just north of Carrigallen in the townland of Drumloona. 'Every place around here is called Drum-something or other. It's all drumlins. They say there was a man called Looney in Drumloona one time. And there's a loony living here still,' says he with a yelp of laughter.

'I can bring the Fitzpatricks back to 1770,' he says. 'My father's name was John. His father was Francis. Then there was Bernard. Then Patrick, like myself, and then Bernard again. They're all buried in the one place in Drumeela, a mile from here.'

Pat was the second of nine children. 'They were all big families around here that time. As the fellow with fifteen children said to the priest, "Well, you see, Father, it's like this, there was three twosomes and two threesomes and one a good many times."'

The memories of his childhood resound with the sound of clogs. 'In the war years – Jaysus, times were tough and nobody had any money – so, what they done is they got soles made out of timber. When the shoe was worn, you brought them to the shoemaker in Newtown Gore – there was another in Carrigallen – and they nailed the leather to the wood. I knew one man who wore them until he died, nothing only clogs. You'd hear him walking forty mile away.'

Pat pulled on his first pair of Wellington boots in 1947. 'That was just after the Big Snow. I know that because I could have done with them before the Big Snow. That was a bad time. The snow blew up into drifts and stayed that way for three solid weeks. There were people with bread vans delivering bread around the country that didn't get home for three weeks. You couldn't move anywhere. My cousins, four hundred yards from here, couldn't get out of their house. For three weeks! Sheep and cattle were dead everywhere. One farmer here lost fifty cattle. He had the whole lot wiped out.'

By the time of the Big Snow, Pat was working full time on the thirty-three-acre family farm to which he ultimately succeeded on the death of his father, aged eighty-four, in 1972, just months after his mother's passing.

Pat proved to be a very capable farmer and was one of the leading lights of Macra na Feirme, the voluntary organisation championing the cause of young farmers, which was founded by science teacher Stephen Cullinan in 1944. One of Pat's most prized photographs is of himself and the six men with whom he won the seven-a-side tug-o-war Macra na Feirme championship in 1958.

One of Macra na Feirme's projects was to encourage farmers to participate in the performing arts. Pat soon discovered he had a taste for the stage and became an actor of some renown in the locality. He is particularly well known for his supporting role in John B. Keane's *Sharon's Grave* where he carried Dinzie Conlee, 'the crippled humpback ferret from hell' for the duration of the play. '"Say nothing till ya hear more,"' whispers Pat. This was a line from *The Run of the Country*, a coming-of-age IRA novel by Shane Connaughton, which was filmed in Redhills, County Cavan, in 1995. Pat had a small role in the film which is probably best known for its vivid depiction of the main character being tarred and feathered. He was also involved with an award-winning 1996 film adaptation of John McGahern's short story *Korea*.

On his kitchen table, Pat keeps a copy of Leland Lewis Duncan's book *The Face of Time: Photographs of County Leitrim, 1862–1923*, which is filled with extraordinary photographs of grim-faced butlers and stoic labourers, tumbling mud houses and women curing goat-skins. 'What do you remark about that?' says Pat of a photograph depicting a large gathering of men. 'Not a bare head in it. Them were the times when no man would leave a house without a hat.'

The Cistercian Monks

Mount Saint Joseph Abbey, Roscrea, County Tipperary

Dom Laurence Walsh (born 1929), Brother Dominic Tobin (born 1925),

Father Ciarán Ó Sabhaois (born 1926), Brother Niall Maguire (born 1914),

Father Éanna Henderson (born 1925), Dom Colmcille O'Toole (born 1925),

Father Robert Kelly (born 1928) & Father Gabriel McCarthy (born 1925)

Dom Laurence Walsh throws thumb and forefinger in the air and whips them back around his chest in a circular manner.

'Um, let's go gardening?' I suggest.

'No,' says he. 'It means: "Cork won by two points."'

The fine art of silent language is something the Cistercians have evolved carefully over the long centuries since Robert of Molesme founded the austere order in 1098. The monks never actually took a vow of silence; a 'general atmosphere of silence' was simply considered essential.

Which is why Dom Laurence, a sporting enthusiast, is so adept at giving scores in sign language.

At the age of eighty-four, Dom Laurence considers himself one of the juniors of Mount St Joseph. He has held numerous roles here over the past six decades including twenty-five years as bursar and three years as abbot. He has also served on and off as prior under four separate abbots.

'I started out as Ned Walsh from Roscrea,' he chuckles. 'My family still know me as Ned. When I came in here, there were a lot of names available because thirty men had just been sent from here to a new foundation in Scotland. I took my father's name. Laurence Walsh. And that's how I am known now. Even my passport calls me Laurence.'

Dom Laurence was an only child. His father, who ran a hardware shop in Roscrea, had often talked about the monks of Mount St Joseph being his greatest customers. 'I always had the priesthood in mind, but not the monastic life,' he says. Although he attended the Cistercian College in Roscrea, right beside the abbey, he had planned to go to St Flannan's College in Ennis.

However, when the president of St Flannan's came to interview Laurence and his father, the fourteen-year-old panicked, hopped up on his bicycle and vanished over the horizon.

'I was going through agony,' he explains. 'I was very happy in the Cistercian College and I didn't want to go to board in Ennis. It was a long way away. When I got back at six o'clock, my father's good name with the clergy was gone and my place at St Flannan's was gone too. So I had to look for some other kind of vocation. I thought of joining the Columban Fathers who were doing a lot of work in China at that time. And then, in my last year – 1946 – I decided to join the monks here.'

Nearly seventy years later, Dom Laurence nimbly guides us through the abbey's church, library, sacristy, refectory, infirmary and college chapel, talking history all the way.

In the seventeenth century, these lands belonged to Dr Richard Heaton, a Yorkshire clergyman regarded as Ireland's first botanist. By 1877, they were purchased by Count Arthur Moore, a wealthy Catholic landowner and Home Rule supporter. He gifted the six hundred-acre property to the Cistercians, including the original mansion and walled garden. The first monks arrived up from the Cistercian abbey of Mount Melleray in County Waterford in February 1878. Working with local stonemasons, the monks then built the magnificent church that stands alongside the college using dark fossil-hued limestone quarried on the land.

Highlights of Mount St Joseph are the stained-glass windows running throughout, depicting the lives of saints and biblical scenes in magnificent colour. Father Richard, the present abbot, was so taken with the windows that, in 2009, he published a beautiful hardback book on them entitled *Lumen Christi*. Dom Laurence wrote the text.

The library boasts a spiral staircase straight out of Hogwarts and is lined with huge, musty old tomes of Latin verse and ancient wisdom. The nearby dormitory, where Dom Laurence slept in the 1940s, has been converted into a library extension, its shelves lined with books written in numerous languages. Their beds comprised of wooden tresses, straw mattresses and pillows of chaff. 'There was great snoring in here at that time,' he laughs, recalling a giant of a man from Limerick. 'He'd barely be in bed and he'd start. I didn't think I'd stick it at all, but actually I got so used to it that I didn't even notice.'

Left to right: Dom Laurence Walsh, Brother Dominic Tobin, Father Ciarán Ó Sabhaois, Brother Niall Maguire, Father Éanna Henderson & Dom Colmcille O'Toole.

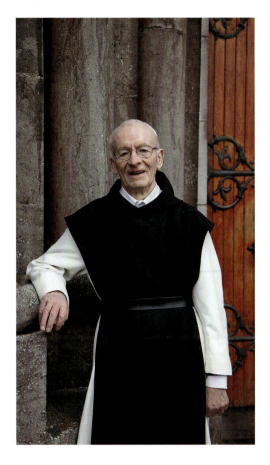

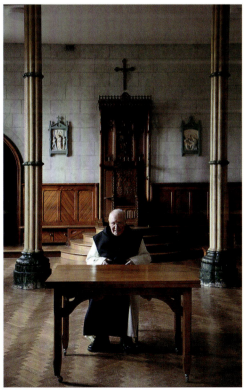

Outside, he points out the dairy farm, the orchard and the walled garden where the monks tend to fruit and vegetables – or, at least, where they did until a combination of old age and supermarkets compelled them to swap their secateurs for a shopping basket.

'There was nearly eighty men here when I first joined,' says Dom Laurence. 'There's nineteen monks resident here now.'

'Is this an interrogation?' asks Dom Colmcille O'Toole, when Dom Laurence lures him in to meet us. 'Oh, well, I'm very photogenic anyway, a beauty at eighty-seven.'

Dom Colmcille is arguably the abbey's most venerable resident, having been elected its abbot in 1964. Born in 1925, he grew up on a small farm in Ballintubber in County Mayo 'where my family of seven brothers had many a fight!' As a boy, he was also educated in the Cistercian College in Roscrea before he joined the order in 1945. During his first year, thirty Cistercian monks from Mount St Joseph founded Sancta Maria Abbey amid the Lammermuir Hills of southern Scotland. It was the first Cistercian house founded in Scotland since the Reformation.

In 1966, Dom Colmcille made a ten-day visitation to the new abbey where his host was Dom Columban Mulcahy, the first abbot of Nunraw. Dom Columban was a son of the former Thurles postmaster and a younger brother of General Richard Mulcahy, Minister for Defence in the Free State Government. 'The general was a very strong character,' says Dom Colmcille. 'An iron heart, totally honest, a man of integrity and I learned a lot from him.'

'The first night I was in Scotland, I was absolutely amazed to think that I was outside of Ireland.' He was destined to travel considerably farther when, in 1965, he went on an extensive visitation to the Cistercian abbeys in New Zealand and Australia. He also played a key role in the foundation at Bolton Abbey near Moone, County Kildare, and made several visitations to another at Mariakloster on the island of Tautra in central Norway where Father Anthony O'Brien of Mount St Joseph serves as chaplain to a community of nine Cistercian nuns.

Opposite page: Father Gabriel McCarthy. Above top: Brother Dominic Tobin. Bottom: Dom Colmcille O'Toole.

At the time of his election as abbot in 1964, Dom Colmcille was only thirty-eight years old and considerably younger than most of the hundred and five monks over whom he presided. 'I was well down on the pecking order of the community. Some of them had even taught me at the college.' However, he rallied to the role and served for an impressive thirty-six years before handing over the reins to Dom Laurence. 'I'm expecting a huge pension any day now,' he says, giving the bursar an ambitious wink.

Dom Laurence says the monks are stirring. They want to know what the two young men with the camera are up to. 'While the ball is on the hop, we may as well make use of it,' he says, and ushers us in to meet the next man.

At the age of eighty-eight, Father Éanna Henderson remains as obsessed with sport as he was eight decades earlier. 'Hurling, football, tennis, soccer, cycling, swimming, the whole lot. I didn't excel at any of them but I loved playing games.' Sport and music were both important parts of his childhood at the Henderson family home in Glasnevin, which was then a small village located on the northern outskirts of Dublin.

There was also rebellion in the blood. A grandmother from Armagh was connected to the Manchester Martyrs, three Irish Fenians hanged for the murder of a British policeman in 1867.

Fifty years later, his father, Frank, and uncle Leo served as officers with the Irish Volunteers. Frank, a printer by trade, was a captain in the GPO garrison during the Easter Rising of 1916 and went on to become Commandant of the Second Battalion of Irish Volunteers.

'They both had links early on to the Gaelic League and to the GAA, the hurling and football. That's how so many people met in those times. They had a common link through sport and music and costume and dancing and the Irish language. That's what bonded them all to Pearse and MacDonagh and Hyde and all of them.'

Father Éanna's other grandmother was known as 'Ma Mór', and was a 'very small and very lovely woman' from County Laois. 'I remember well the time that she was brought down here by one of the family. Even though she was ninety-two years of age, she hopped out of the car like a girl and when Father Oliver gave her a bowl of strawberries and ice cream, she was as happy as anything. That was the last time I ever saw her.'

Brother Dominic Tobin, who was born in 1925, was nineteen years old when he joined the order. Having grown up on a farm beside Mount Melleray Abbey in the Knockmealdown Mountains, he naturally gravitated towards the abbey farm. He has subsequently served as farm manager for over thirty years, primarily overseeing the dairy herd that supplies milk to the Avonmore creamery.

Father Ciarán Ó Sabhaois, born in 1926, is a passionate Irish speaker who grew up on a small farm near Newry in south Armagh. 'And the first lesson of education is to grow up on a small farm,' he counsels. Having traced his Savage, or Ó Sabhaois, ancestry back to the Normans, his interest in matters historical ensured his appointment as the abbey archivist. He maintains that the change has been minimal since he joined the order in 1948. 'There were more people,' he says. 'It was a lot stricter and you could only communicate by signs. But otherwise it was the same as it is now.'

Brother Niall Maguire, now ninety-nine, was in his sixties when he joined the order, having previously worked as a Revenue Commissioner. However, most of the monks who reside at Mount St Joseph arrived before the Second Vatican Council convened under Pope John XXIII in 1962. Better known as Vatican II, the Council sought to reform the Church and reconnect it with the post-war world of the 1960s.

In Roscrea, the monks no longer say mass in Latin, which didn't initially appeal to Dom Laurence. 'I opposed it when it started,' says he, 'but looking back after so many years, I can see it was very necessary. I just couldn't see that at the time.' Incidentally, Dom Laurence is now an internet-savvy octogenarian.

Vatican II also enabled the order to open up to Roscrea a little more although Dom Colmcille maintains

that they are still more enclosed as an order than others. 'You can feel yourself being drawn out sometimes,' he says, 'so you need some strength to resist it.'

The jury is still out as to whether or not the corridors of Mount St Joseph became any noisier after Vatican II. The return of the voice had to be weighed against the ever-diminishing number of monks walking through the abbey every passing year.

'Very few enter nowadays,' concedes Dom Laurence. 'Our two juniors are in their forties. One is approaching Final Profession and the other has recently completed his training. Richard, our abbot, is the youngest monk of all at thirty-seven years of age.'

Before we leave, I ask Father Ciarán how you tell someone you're in a bad mood in Cistercian sign language. There is a momentary silence broken only by the ticking of umpteen clocks on the walls. With the other monks watching on, he gamely places his knuckles on his chest and rubs them with a silent snarl. The room duly reverberates with the sound of ancient laughter.

Opposite page: Brother Dominic Tobin (left), Father Robert Kelly (right). Above: Dom Laurence. Previous spread: Dom Laurence Walsh (left), Father Robert Kelly (right).

Sonny Egan

Ferbane, County Offaly

Hackney Driver and Farmer

Born 1932

'I have a theory as to why Kerry won their thirty-six All-Ireland titles. It's because of all the lovely beaches down there. It's No Man's Land! You could run along Inch beach all day and still not get to the end of it. That's why the feckers won the All-Ireland. If Offaly had beaches, we'd win more All-Irelands. But we've no beaches!'

Sonny is something of a Gaelic football enthusiast – 'I'm mad on football, it's the only game' – and for all his talk of beaches, he still rates Kerry's Mick O'Connell as the greatest player of all time. 'He had such style,' marvels Sonny. 'He was a beautiful kicker, pinpoint accuracy. And he had a bit of madness too. When he was training, he threw himself up in the air, as high as he could, and then he'd whop himself down on the ground, the full length, so he'd get used to falling. I would say he went to the very limits of endurance.'

Sonny is an only child, as was his mother before him. Christened Mary Bridget Cantwell, she descended from Thomas de Kentewall, an Anglo-Norman crusader who served alongside the Butlers of Kilkenny during the twelfth century. Known as Cantwell Fada, or Long Cantwell, Thomas' tomb in Kilfane, County Kilkenny, is engraved with an image of a tall, slender knight in chain mail, brandishing a shield bedecked with the Cantwell coat of arms. 'Long Cantwell?' says Sonny, taking stock of his own height. 'Well, I didn't take after him so!'

The Cantwells fell from grace when they refused to conform to the Protestant faith in the seventeenth century. A branch of the family subsequently established itself at Clara, County Offaly, from which sprang John Cantwell who, as Bishop of Meath, was one of the key figures in Irish Catholicism during the mid-nineteenth century.

Sonny's mother's family hailed from Kilcolgan More, close to the Offaly–Westmeath border. The road on which they lived was known as Cantwell Street because there were so many of them there. Her father, Tom Cantwell, had the rather formidable circumstance of being an only son with eleven sisters. 'Fourteen in the one house and only two of them men,' declares Sonny in sympathetic awe.

In 1928, Mary Cantwell married John Egan who hailed from a hundred-acre farm on the slopes of Endrim Hill, just northwest of Ferbane. Born in 1898, John was the son of another John Egan and his wife Sarah Leonard from Killoughey parish near Kinnitty. 'Nearly all the marriages were arranged in my grandfather's time and maybe in my father's time too,' says Sonny. 'Love didn't play in those times. Love wouldn't put bread on the table!'

Following Tom Cantwell's death, John and Mary Egan moved to Kilcolgan and took over the farm where young Sonny grew up. He went to school in Ballyclare, west of Ferbane, a five-mile trek from Kilcolgan.

In 1962, he began working part-time for Bord na Móna, initially digging drains and tapping the bog at Boora, later 'graduating' to driving machines to mill and harvest the peat. 'We were delighted when the machines came,' he says. 'It took all the hardship out of it. Before that, we had to work so hard to get the work done manually. And then there were machines to cut the hay and harvest the corn and cut the turf. That was brilliant, in my opinion.'

Sonny spent just three years with Bord na Móna but speaks fondly of his time on the bogs. 'The crew I was working with were brilliant. All auld country lads from different parishes in an area about twenty miles round. Most of them had small farms so the fellows that didn't have farms would be ribbing the ones that did. The craic was ninety at the tea breaks.'

'We were all so fit then,' he says reflectively. 'God we were flying. We could go out through stone walls.' Sonny kept himself in robust shape by playing his beloved football as often as he could. He played on the Ferbane minor team when they defeated Clara to win the county championship in 1949. He was also on the junior team that won the 1952 championship, beating Doon, and the intermediate team that won both the 1957 and 1959 county championships, beating Kilcormac and Gracefield respectively.

After he left Bord na Móna, Sonny teamed up with Mick Moore from a neighbouring farm. 'We'd often do a week's work together, manual labour, making hay and things. One of us would have the hay rake with the horse yoked up to it. The other fellow would have the two-pronged fork and he'd be making the cocks of hay out of it. Trams of hay, that's what we called the round bundles.'

Sometimes Mick and Sonny joined forces with other small farmers to help draw in the corn or hay. 'There might be ten or twelve men making the ricks and then there'd be twenty men at the threshing after that. The craic was mighty. There'd be porter going, spilling and everything, the middle of the day. It was fierce dirty, thirsty work so maybe you'd get a bottle on the hour. You had to be careful though because the belts on the tractor that were powering the threshing mill were deadly dangerous. You wouldn't be long getting gobbled up. It was a fierce machine with rotating teeth. An awesome-looking thing, worse than a lion's mouth to look into. If you put in your hand, you were gone.'

Away from the sports field, the cornfields and the peat bogs, Sonny liked to party. 'We worked hard and we played hard,' he says. 'I ate and drank and I done everything under the sun. I lived life to the full, yes – and sometimes it nearly flowed over.'

Sonny was one of the first in the parish to own a car, a Hillman Minx. During the late 1950s and early 1960s, he and his pals would drive down to Dublin city in pursuit of 'the women and the beer and all the new films'.

'Ah, we had a great life,' he says. 'For four years solid, there was hardly a Sunday when we didn't drive to Dublin. We saw films like *The Sound of Music* three months before anyone up here saw them. We were way ahead of the posse, that's the gospel truth!' Lengthy refreshments tended to follow the movie, and 'we'd drive home and distribute the passengers at about seven or eight in the morning'.

Sonny took over the farm on his father's death in 1970. However, he quickly decided farming was not for him. 'I could see no future in it so I pulled out.' As a youngster, he had once spent a Sunday chauffeuring his neighbours around in the Hillman – to mass, to relations, to a match in Portlaoise. At the end of the day, he had made £26, which compared favourably to the £6 a week he was paid at Bord na Móna.

In the mid-1970s, Sonny reinvented himself as a hackney driver. By then he'd traded in the Hillman for a Morris Minor. 'It was a scream,' he says of his hackney years. 'You'd be meeting all kinds of characters and hearing all kinds of stories, good and bad. I once drove a man to Cork city. You couldn't go any farther unless you had wings.'

There were scary nights too, like the time he had to take a minibus full of brandy-swilling ruffians from Kilbeggan to Mullingar. 'They were the biggest desperadoes you ever could come across, punching women and everything.' But he has happy memories too, such as his frequent encounters with an old cattle drover called John Joe Gannon, 'the nicest old man you could meet'. John Joe told Sonny that he averaged fifty or sixty miles a day, every day of the week. 'And he was so fit that he was still gliding when he was ninety. Flying it! Lord, I used to envy him!'

In 1970, Sonny went to a dance in Mullingar and met Agnes Olwill, a nurse from Seeharan, near Virginia, County Cavan. The couple were married in Cross, Mullagh, County Cavan, and they settled in Breehoge, just north of the Cantwell farm of Kilcolgan, where they raised four children. The view from their kitchen window affords an unbroken stretch over a series of nine-acre fields to the Slieve Bloom Mountains.

Sonny still enjoys a night out, although he admits he doesn't sing quite as often as he used to. 'I'd sing forty years ago all right. I'd have to have forty pints before I started and well, then you couldn't stop me.' He had enjoyed a lively session shortly before our encounter and estimated that it would be 'another month' before he was fully recovered.

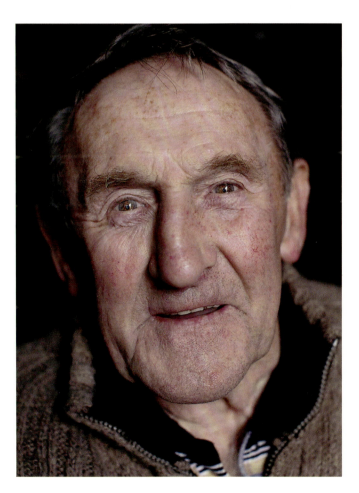

Máirtín Nee

Cashel, County Galway

Bar Manager and Connemara Pony Breeder

Born 1941

In the summer of 1905, a thirty-one-year-old Irish-Italian engineer alighted from a train in Recess with a plan. Guglielmo Marconi was the second son of a wealthy Bolognese landowner. His mother was a Jameson from the whiskey distilling family. It was Marconi's intention to build a radio station in Connemara from where he hoped to pioneer wireless contact with North America.

Today, Marconi is credited as the man who effectively made radio mainstream, winning a Nobel Prize in 1909. But when Máirtín Nee's grandfather and namesake met the Italian at the station in Recess, Marconi was still an unknown entity.

'My grandfather brought him and all his bits and pieces from Recess out here to Cashel,' says Máirtín. 'He was working here with his horse and cart and he took Marconi all around. They started across the road at Lehenagh where he got a small sort of a tingle on the radio. He went from there to Errisbeg, the hill over Roundstone, and he tried again up behind Josie Keaney's house in Canower. He got a great signal at Errisbeg but he needed a lake for earthing, so he went on west.'

At length, Marconi settled on the three-hundred-acre Derrygimla bog, three miles south of Clifden, where he was able to direct his aerial straight across the ocean to Glace Bay, Newfoundland. A regular trans-Atlantic radio-telegraph service commenced in 1907. 'Have I done the world good or have I added a menace?' Marconi would later wonder.

Máirtín is well versed on the subject of Marconi. He has always known that his grandfather was once the great inventor's chauffeur. When Marconi's daughter, Princess Elettra Marconi, came to visit Connemara for the radio's centenary celebrations in 2007, Máirtín got the call up to collect her. The Chamber of Commerce had the original trap in which Marconi had travelled 102 years earlier, and it was down to Máirtín to provide the Connemara pony and harness. He duly escorted Princess Elettra and her son, Prince Guglielmo, to Clifden for the celebrations.

Máirtín is a well-known breeder of Connemara ponies, the hardy breed which originated in this broad and beautiful peninsula. 'I rear them and I breed them and I sell them anywhere I can,' he explains. His signature cowboy hat and pipe have made him a famous sight at shows all over Ireland.

It all began in 1953 when, aged twelve, he cycled seventeen miles to Maam Cross with £10 in his pocket. 'I bought a foal for £7-10 from the Mannions of Rosmuc. And I was so proud that the road wasn't wide enough for me and my foal coming home.'

That foal was the first of over a hundred ponies Máirtín has owned in the ensuing six decades, not to mention the scores he has bought and sold on behalf of other people. Many of his own have carried the name 'Doonreaghan' in honour of his home place near Cashel. Doonreaghan Marty, for instance, a yearly colt sired by Coolillaun Cushlawn (owned by Eamonn Burke) won his class at the 2010 All-Ireland Championship in Oldcastle, County Meath.

He allows a smile for a handsome colt he sold to a German which was named Máirtín in his honour, and he is proud of a stallion bred in Cork which he turned into a Grade A showjumper. 'I trained him how to jump as high as any horse and he can now take on the best of them.'

Máirtín also trains his ponies for driving competitions, slaloming between cones, and he won the All-Ireland in 2006. He used to ride them himself but believes he is now too aged for such carry-on.

A man with a keen eye for quality, Máirtín speaks in short, concise sentences. Considering all the foals and fillies he has bought and sold, he retains an extraordinary memory for detail, rattling off sizes and sires, dams and dates, with the same nonchalant manner that he pours an exquisite pint of stout.

Máirtín is no amateur at pouring a pint. For twenty-one years and seven months, he worked at the Zetland House Hotel on the edge of Cashel Bay. Built as a shooting lodge in 1856, this handsome building was named for the earls of Zetland, one of whom was Viceroy of Ireland from 1888 to 1890. In the early twentieth century, Johnny O'Loughlin, the local school teacher, turned the building into a Connemara institution, establishing it as a shop and a bar, and later as a hotel. By the time Máirtín began working there, the hotel was owned by the Guinness Brewery.

'I started off as a porter and I ended up as the bar manager,' he says. The bar was replete with snugs in the tradition of the old style, while the shop served all the basic groceries required by the local community. The shop and the snugs have disappeared but the walls are still lined with photographs of characters from the good old days. Máirtín knew them well, the ghillies and boatmen and fishermen, many of whom were born in the nineteenth century.

'I used to spend hours and hours talking with the old people,' he says. 'I found them awful interesting. But when they're gone, they're gone, and what they know goes with them.'

Máirtín grew up in Lehenagh, where he was the third of seven children. His father, Johnny Nee, worked at the hotel for the O'Neill family who owned it before Guinness. Johnny spent his days gardening, milking the cows and making hay. When he was young, Máirtín would count anything up to sixty Galway hookers out in the bay. Three of his sisters emigrated to Chicago in the 1950s and early 1960s, though two of them subsequently returned to Ireland. His brother and other two sisters have always lived in Cashel.

Although he spent three weeks in Chicago, Máirtín was never tempted to leave Ireland. Connemara is where he has lived his life. It's also where he met his wife, Mary Conroy, who was working as a waitress at the Zetland. They were married in 1968, the same year that former French President, Charles de Gaulle, called into the Zetland while staying as a guest at nearby Cashel House.

Máirtín and Mary have two sons and two daughters. They now live in Doonreaghan, a few minutes' walk from the Zetland, in a house that overlooks Bertraghboy Bay with Glinsk on the far horizon.

Seamus Vaughan

Upper Dirreen, Athea, County Limerick

Clothes Merchant and Turf Cutter

Born 1922

'My father had a great pair of legs. I was able to waltz okay, but I wasn't any good at the step-dancing.'

Seamus' father, Joe Vaughan, was a slim and agile man who worked as a ganger with Limerick County Council, but his true passion was step-dancing. He was one of the finest step-dancing teachers in County Limerick and his fame spread across the Atlantic to New York. 'I had a brother, Jack, who was a great dancer in America,' says Seamus. 'And my daughter, Áine, was a fine dancer too.'

Shortly after the end of the First World War, Joe met and married Margaret Ahern, a fellow native of west Limerick. They had both lost their fathers young – Joe's father died aged forty-four with a burst appendix and Margaret's father Paddy Ahern was killed in a quarry accident in Dirreen while digging for flagstones.

During the War of Independence, Joe served in the Irish Republican Army. Many young men from this area had been stunned when Con Colbert of nearby Athea became the youngest of the Easter Rising leaders to be executed in 1916. Seamus, apolitical himself, does not know whether his father saw any action but he mentions that a nearby bridge was strategically blown up at the height of the war. In later years, Joe served with the Local Defence Force.

Like the Irish Free State itself, Seamus was born in 1922. 'When I was to be baptised, I was taken in an ass and cart to the village. I suppose people would pay good money to go to a baptism in an ass and cart these days.'

He went to school at Knocknagortna, a four-mile walk from his childhood home. The young Vaughans would march barefoot across the fields, carrying sods of turf and bottles of tea. All the bottles were lined up around the school fire so that the tea would be nicely warmed up for the children by lunchtime.

From school he went to work for a local farmer. Seamus was always strong on mathematics. As such, he wasn't thrilled when, after twelve months of hard work on the farm, he totted up his total earnings to fourteen shillings.

Seamus decided enough was enough, handed in his notice and, one way or another, joined the British army. The Second World War was in motion but, although he was sent to France, young Seamus was spared from any action. One of his most lasting memories was looking up at the skies over Brittany and watching the Wellington bombers returning from a night assault on Germany.

After the war, he briefly served in the Irish army and was stationed at the Curragh Camp in County Kildare. On one occasion, he served the final meal to one of the last men hanged in Ireland. 'You eat it,' said the condemned man. 'You'll need it more than I will.'

Army life was not for Seamus either. He was increasingly inclined to think that there was only one person in the world from whom he should be taking orders – and that was himself.

He made his way to the Bog of Allen and began harvesting turf. Now he just needed a way to get the turf from the bog to the customer. At this point, he became close friends with Joe Burns, an Ulster-born turf dealer living in Newcastle West. Joe taught Seamus how to drive and inspired his keen understanding of the turf industry. And perhaps, most importantly, he lent Seamus a Bedford truck with which he could distribute his turf from the Bog of Allen.

Turf became his foremost business. 'I was carrying turf to people all around. I was selling it by the lorry load. I took it to Limerick city and Kildorrery and all parts of County Cork. Everyone around this side of the country made money from the turf at that time. That is the way it was.'

By 1951, Seamus had made enough money from the turf to buy a Hillman as well as his own truck. 'I insured my first lorry for £9 and my last for £1,000,' he marvels. Seamus would become famous in west Limerick when he ran an unofficial bus service to Sunday mass in Athea. He would set off from home in the lorry and gradually collect more and more people, putting the elderly up in the cab alongside him, with everyone else – his children included – standing in the back, holding onto the rails. By the time he got to church, he sometimes had as many as thirty people in the lorry.

The Hillman was also sometimes recruited for ecclesiastical service. On one occasion he carried the coffin of a deceased relative, strapped to the roof, on behalf of an undertaker whose hearse was out of action.

During the course of his travels, he met and married

Mary Sheehan, a fluent Irish speaker, whose parents ran a small grocery from their home in nearby Kilbaha. Seamus and Mary had thirteen children, eight girls and five boys.

Margaret, their eldest daughter, was born in 1953. She says her father always managed to bring home enough money to ensure that there was plenty of food on the table and clothes to wear.

Indeed, if Seamus' lorry wasn't full of turf, it was invariably stuffed with clothes. A considerable supply of these came from Clery's department store on O'Connell Street in Dublin. Seamus' sister, Eileen, was married to John Joe Collins, a nephew of Denis Guiney, the Kerry draper who bought Clery's in 1941 and converted it into one of the biggest success stories of post-war Dublin. A photograph of Eileen and John Joe's wedding hangs proudly on Seamus' wall.

Throughout the 1960s and 1970s, Seamus would power up to Dublin in his lorry, fill it with clothes from Clery's and then make his way back to Munster. 'I'd be selling all sorts of clothes, wherever I could sell them,' he recalls fondly. 'At the fairs and markets, anywhere. I went down into Kerry and up into Clare, Ennistymon and such like. It's full of Vaughans up in Clare.'

'When Daddy was in the rag trade, we got the best of what was going,' adds Margaret wistfully. 'We were always beautifully dressed in Clery's finest!'

'I'm sure there were difficult times,' she adds, 'but we certainly never felt like we were poor. Killing the pig was a big day. We'd bring all the best pork steak around to the neighbours so that when they killed their pig, they'd bring the best back to us. We ate a lot of trout from the river, which my uncle, Tom Sheehan, would catch. Sometimes, we'd have rabbit or pheasant. And I remember we had goat kid one time too which I wasn't mad about.'

As the family grew in size, so the Vaughan family home was extended this way and that. 'Daddy would say that he earned more money than anyone in County Limerick,' says Margaret, 'and that he spent it as well.'

In the early 1980s, Seamus had a bad accident at Ferry Bridge. 'And I didn't drive the lorry any more after that.' He did continue on in a van, selling fruit and vegetables, and he also continued to be involved in the turf trade. On one occasion, he went to visit a farmer outside Listowel to enquire about purchasing some turf. The farmer told him that he was emigrating to America the following week, with his wife and six children, and asked Seamus if he knew anyone who might buy his land. That evening, Seamus arrived home to his family and told them that, for £600, he was now the owner of a small farm outside Listowel.

Mary passed away in 2011 but Seamus still has plenty of family in the neighbourhood. He is particularly proud as a father because the entrepreneurial gene has so evidently made its way through to the next generation.

'I've done every kind of a job. Collecting turf, drawing turnips, selling clothes. I had a go at everything. It's simple. If you worked for a farmer, it would take you a month to earn a pound. If you worked for yourself, you could earn quicker. Every one of my sons is working for themselves now.'

Sonaí Choilm Learaí Ó Conghaile

Coradh Bhuí, Leitir Mealláin, Contae na Gaillimhe

Melodeon Player and Fisherman

Born 1945

'Now, there is still music here,' concedes Sonaí. 'But I'm sorry to tell you it's the wrong music. There is only one family playing traditional music in this part of Connemara now and that is my own family.'

Nóra enters the room with the tea, and listens to her husband of forty years as he lambasts the gyrating temptations of 'disco music' that has compelled younger generations to abandon melodeons and fiddles in favour of a boogie.

'He's mad every day with it,' she explains patiently.

'I am not blaming the musicians,' continues Sonaí. 'Everyone has to make a few shilling. But I am blaming the pubs that won't give the trad musicians a chance to show people how it's done and how it's played.'

The Ó Conghaile family have been in the Leitir Mealláin (Lettermullen) area since records began, although Sonaí's father was the only one of eight children who did not settle in either Chicago or Pennsylvania.

Their household at Coradh Bhuí has always been Irish-speaking and musical. 'My father and all his sisters and brothers, my mother, my aunts … they were all singers and dancers,' says Sonaí. 'It was never competitive, mind. It wasn't like they'd be out in a rowing boat, one trying to beat the other. They'd dance and sing and maybe they'd take a drink and they'd sing a song together. My father was a great sean-nós dancer when he had a few glasses of poitín on him.'

The symptoms were unsurprisingly genetic. 'Music was always in my head,' says Sonaí. 'I was no good at school – myself and the teacher weren't very healthy anyhow – but music, music.'

Sonaí was eight when he first took up the melodeon. And the one that he took up wasn't his. 'A fellow used to come here because his father would not let him play at home. He'd play until maybe eleven o'clock at night and when he left, he would put the accordion up on the dresser until the following night. I would be dying till he'd go home and, when he was gone, I'd take it down. I was watching his fingers and the way he moved them. And when I got the accordion, I started playing and playing. And from that day on, I got into music. I played melodeon at my first wedding when I was fourteen years old. And the fellow who got married was Jimmy Ó Domhnaill, and he and his wife are still alive. Ask him, "Who played at your wedding, Jimmy?" and see what he says.'

In September 1962, like so many a Connemara boy, he packed an old suitcase and made his way to London where he was soon 'digging trenches and muck and sweating for Murphy and McAlpine and all them'. After work, he and his pals would head to the pub 'instead of having water' and make some new friends. 'We'd have a game of darts and cards and some laughs and next thing you're there till eleven o'clock. Up in the morning and go again'.

He became part of the London Irish, living it up at The Shamrock and the Galtymore dancehall in Cricklewood, and playing melodeon at pubs and clubs all over the city.

'You could never do anything like that here because there was no money here. If you came home for a couple of weeks in the summertime, you'd have the craic. But it was only yourself that was making that craic – it wasn't there before you.'

So it was fortunate indeed that come 1964 he chanced upon a young Connemara beauty called Nora Ní Mhaoláin. They met at a Christmas dance at the hall in Tír an Fhia, a mile over the bridge from Lettermore. Nóra had also gone to England where she'd been working at a hospital in Huddersfield. Much impressed by the girl, Sonaí applied his characteristically audacious gusto to invite her father to come home with him instead of her.

'There was no flies on him, only dead ones,' interjects Nóra drolly.

The couple dated for four years, then returned home to marry in Galway city in 1968. Three weeks after the birth of their first son, Michael, they returned to London for another four years. They fetched up with six children, three boys and three girls. Sonaí had long since given up the drink to focus on making money.

As such, when they returned to live in south Galway, the challenge was to find an income from a landscape that had grown wild in their absence. 'When the old people were here, there was always someone to look after everything. There were hens and the goose and the gander, cattle and sheep, and the land was always clear. But when my generation went to London working, we

forgot our own village, our own house, and, by the time we got back, everything had gone wild. Even the fields were full of bracken and briars.'

Sonaí became a fisherman, setting off in his currach around Golan Head, looking for lobster and crayfish. 'I never took any liberty against the sea water,' says he, 'because she's there, she's the boss. So I go out and make sure my motor is all right and that I have an anchor.'

Nonetheless, he's had several close shaves. One cold October morning, he and his son, Michael, who was fourteen at the time, took the currach out to investigate an oil tanker that had come aground on the rocks the night before. The sea was still rough and black with oil from the stricken ship. 'As I was bending down, a big bucket slips off the seat and bangs Michael, who's steering. He slipped out the back, the boat flipped around and I went out the side. Luckily the lock was on the engine and it was going around and around. I could see the propellers spinning. I stretched out my hand and caught her while she was going around and I pulled myself in.' Michael was still adrift, sinking into the oily swell in his oilskins, but Sonaí managed to take control of his vessel and sailed to the rescue. 'And from that day until this, Michael was never in the sea again,' says he.

On another occasion, the rope he was pulling to restart the engine snapped and he tipped back into the heavy seas, unbeknownst to his fellow sailor. When he resurfaced, covered in sand, he was already six yards from the boat, the distance growing with every second. But the gods were good and hurled the boat back his way, he caught the side and managed to scramble up the sides. 'The worst moment is when your feet are slipping on the side of the boat.'

There was also a dark moment on a sunny Sunday morning when he was returning from a review of some cattle he kept on a nearby island. A black bag floating alongside the pier caught his eye and he called to a friend on the pier to help get it out. As his friend reached for the bag, it rolled over in the water and that's when Sonaí realised it was not a bag but a body, 'and 'twas the face of a man I knew, Lord have mercy on him.'

Back on shore, Sonaí and the kids would amble through the limestone boulders and granite rocks at low tide, digging for clams, razorfish and shellfish. Or else they would simply scoop up seaweed to bring to the factory in Kilkieran – red dillisk and carrageen moss, scarlet ribbon weed, purple laver and brown kelp.

'Everyone was fishing that time, but now that's all gone. If you sold a load of seaweed or moss now, the social welfare man would come after you and want to know how much did you sell. That's what killed it for me. And that is why everyone is sitting down now even though there's plenty of work to be done. Why would they do anything if the social welfare man will take the money off them? So we don't earn money to spend money and now there is no market for anything.'

The air in Coradh Bhuí is brisk and invigorating but it has never been an easy place to live.

'I see young fellows who are coming older now and I feel sorry for them because they're going the same way. They're on the pier and there's nothing for them to do here and no place to go. So, just as we did, they must go away.'

Bill and Birdie Martin

Mullaghmast, County Kildare

Cattle Breeders

Born 1921 & 1931

'The missus gets up at six in the morning,' marvels Bill Martin.

'I'm never in bed any later than that,' agrees Birdie.

'And I tell you, when she gets up, she opens this window and that window and every window in the house, so that you either get up or perish in the bed!'

'And do you get up then, Daddy?' asks Birdie in mock indignation. Bill is not her father – he is her husband and has been for the past forty-eight years – but she calls him Daddy all the same.

'Well, to tell the truth, no,' concedes Bill. 'She'll bring me down a warm cup of tea to the bed at eight o'clock in the morning.'

'Seven. Seven. Seven.' She says it three times, eyes raised, as if she has said it a million times.

'Seven? Jaysus, does it be as early as that? I don't be well awake at that hour, you know. My eyes would only be opening up.'

'And I'm doing that for nearly half a century now,' says she.

'That's the truth,' he concludes.

Bill and Birdie are as charming a couple as you can meet. There is much laughter and camaraderie between them. Birdie is constantly flicking his ears and play-boxing him in the ribs. They still flirt and rile and tease and torment and love each other, just as they did back in the early 1960s when Bill first offered to walk her home from a dance in Crookstown. 'He asked me after only one waltz,' says Birdie, still bashful at his haste. 'I didn't know what I was getting into, mind! He was my first and only one.'

Bill was born in 1921 when Ireland was still part of the British Empire. Birdie Dempsey arrived a decade later. Both came from a farming background. The Martins have been in and around the Quaker village of Ballitore for innumerable generations. Bill's grandfather drove dray-loads of straw north from Ballitore to the British cavalry horses stationed at the Curragh. One sad day, shortly before the First World War, he was tying a load of straw when a rope snapped and the straw came tumbling down upon him in such volume that he was crushed to death.

Ned Martin, Bill's father, succeeded to the family home, a labourer's cottage built by the Land Commission in 1912. He rented it for one or two shillings a week. The Land Commission also assigned Ned and three of his neighbours a quarter share each in a thirty-two-acre plot of land known as the Cow Park where their cattle would graze in a communal manner.

Ned worked as a ploughman for farmers in the area, such as the Fennells of Burtown House and the Butterfields of Ballitore. He married Anne Leigh and had three sons and a daughter.

'I left school when I was twelve year old,' says Bill, who was the youngest son. 'And I started picking stones and potatoes for old Jim Fennell at Burtown. I knew him well. He had got an awful shock in the war. He and his wife, Cynthia, would come up every day on their two horses and ride around and see everything that was going on. I worked there eighteen years after that, pulling the horses and ploughing and tilling the land. There was twelve men at it full time, with maybe fifteen or more when the crops would come on to be saved. All the people from Ballitore would come in, snagging turnips, snagging beet, picking potatoes. There were no eleven o'clock breaks in those times,' says he, shaking his head at the very thought of the idea. 'You'd get the work done. And you'd bring your lunch in with you. A bit of bread and butter – if you had butter.'

Cattle were his forte and he often herded them down the back roads to the fairs in Dunlavin and Baltinglass. 'I remember the slaughter of the calves too, when there was no market for them. A man came around to shoot them all. You'd get seven and sixpence a time once you proved they were buried.'

'There were six work and cart horses in Burtown one time, and a couple of hunters. Sometimes we'd be carrying big barrels – fourteen stone of barley, sixteen stone of wheat – out on a pony and dray to the threshing mill in Athgarvan. That journey would take you a whole day at that time.'

Perhaps the sweetest sound you could hear back then was the evening bell that rang out across the fields from Burtown at 6 p.m. to let everyone know the day's work was done. 'The bell was so high up that we could all hear it but, oh God yes, we would listen out for it all right.'

It wasn't all farming, though. Bill had a wandering disposition that took him to faraway Munster where he drove bulldozers around the Devil's Bit and helped lay the runway along the bog that enabled Shannon airport to open for business in 1945. 'A rolling stone gathers no moss,' says he, 'but I have travelled all over Ireland.'

He subsequently fine-tuned his zest for travel into a passion for horse-racing. 'Don't mention racing to me!' he chuckles. 'I was about eight year old when I went first to the Curragh, my first meeting, on a Saturday. And I have been there at nearly every meeting since. And I go to Galway, Gowran, Leopardstown, Punchestown, the lot. I know all those racing crowds. They were always very good to me, to tell you the truth.'

At one such meeting, a cameraman photographed him standing alongside Michael O'Leary, an immense supporter of Irish horse-racing. The Ryanair chief turned to Bill afterwards and said, 'Come on and I'll take you for a flight.'

'"Jaysus, you won't,"' says I, '"I'll keep me feet on the ground."'

'Another time I was up in the Curragh, watching the auld horses going around. There was a smashing-looking lady beside me. Very good looking and I was chatting her up. She didn't know me, you know. Anyway, the horses were going down to the ring. And then this lad come over and took a snap of the two of us for a paper. And she says, "Jesus, Mary and Joseph, I'm a nurse and I'm supposed to be on sick leave – what will I do!?" She was nearly passing out ...'

'And he was ready to give her the kiss of life,' interjects Birdie.

'... so', continues Bill, 'I told her I'd tell him to leave it out. "No," she says, "I'll take a chance. Leave it be." A fortnight's time, a niece brings me the paper. Me and the nurse. They gave me a hundred pound for it. I don't know what the nurse got for it.'

Bill and Birdie have three sons and several grandchildren, including a toddler called Ben whom they were looking after on the day we visited. 'You're a lad who can fight for what you want, ain't you, Ben?' says his grandfather, kicking a ball over at him. 'And you only a babby.'

In later years, the Martins reared Charolais cattle which they exhibited at shows around the area, including Tullow, Athy, Tinahely and Tullamore. Birdie shows us a photo of Mullaghmast Mabel, a Tullow Show award winner in 1996.

'Ah, we'd wash her and get her ready, the two of us … ' recalls Bill, trailing off as he feels Birdie looking at him. 'Well, it was the missus …'

'We showed her in three of four categories and she came second in them all,' says Birdie factually. 'So I said, "Let me wash that coat and I'll bring her around for the last one." I washed her down and we went into a class with twenty-five other cows, and we won. And I was always washing cattle after that. Sometimes I'd be up at four o'clock in the morning to wash a cow before the show.'

'Mabel won first prizes all over the country, but she bred no calves,' says Bill, looking closely at the photograph. 'But of course we Irish are great complainers.'

'We're never satisfied,' agrees Birdie. 'If we're not growling about the weather, we're growling about money.'

Jimmy Ryan

Crosscannon, Killenaule, County Tipperary

Hurley Maker

Born 1928

'I suppose I'm the only man alive who can say he made a hurley for Christy Ring. Ah, they can say what they like about hurlers of the present, but there was never a man like Christy Ring and never will be. And, do you know, I made a hurley for Christy Ring and for John Doyle and for Jimmy Doyle. They had twenty-three All-Ireland's between them. Isn't that some going?'

Jimmy Ryan is in reminiscent form as he sweeps the swirling shavings on his workshop floor into a crisp, immaculate pile. The room is exceptionally orderly, despite the fact that it is business as usual on the morning of our visit. There are hurleys in various stages of progress all around the workshop. At one end, the blocks of ash from which he will create the initial shape. At the other, the completed hurleys, neatly stacked along one wall, with the smaller, children's hurleys lined up along the window sill above them.

'To make the perfect hurley, you need an ash tree that is between twenty-five and thirty-five years old. If the tree is any younger than that, you won't get enough hurleys out of it. And if the tree has gone beyond thirty-five, then the skin becomes too rough and the timber is old and brittle.'

Jimmy has been making hurleys since he was a young man. Carpentry was in his blood. 'The first hurley I ever had was made by my uncle with a big axe and a plane and broken glass to finish it off. I adored that hurley. Then a big bully came and broke it on me. I cried, but the bully lad just laughed.'

Shortly after he left school, Jimmy began attending woodwork nightclasses in Killenaule. 'I made my first hurley under the direction of the woodwork teacher. I had no tools, but he had them all. I was very proud of that hurley. The first one I ever made.'

Jimmy claims he has no head for keeping records and cannot contemplate how many hurleys he has actually made down through the decades. 'If they were all put end to end, I'd say they would go the ninety miles to Croke Park and most of the way back again,' says he. He is famed in the locality for making hurleys for young fellows and refusing to accept payment. The quickest one he made took nine and a half minutes, although he reckons a rate of three hurleys an hour is acceptable going.

'I even made hurleys for some lads over in Milwaukee. They weren't affiliated to the GAA, but they used to have their own competition on Sundays. They came over here to get them and we had a good old night inside

the house after. They invited Mary and I back to Milwaukee for Irish Craft Week, everything free from the gate in. But it clashed! It was the same week as my fiftieth All-Ireland, so I couldn't go.'

Jimmy concedes that he was in the doghouse with Mary for 'about three weeks afterwards' when the Milwaukee holiday fell through, but says he had a record to maintain. 'I saw sixty-three All-Ireland hurling finals and I have not missed one since 1949 when Tipp beat Laois, 3–13 to 3 points. And I had fifty-six football All-Irelands stacked up as well. All consecutive. Nothing in between. The first I saw was Cavan and Mayo in 1948.'

'There is such an atmosphere at Croke Park. Everyone nearly shaking hands with you. I loved to go up on the train because there was such chat, all the old fellows talking. When I was a young man, I thought everyone else was old. But I took the train up with Mary and the boys too, when they were very small, running around the carriages. The train was packed and we'd all have seats in different places – one time I sat on the edge of a table 'but I loved every minute of it. I got to see some great men playing – and a lot of them ended up in the Dáil.' Jimmy says his father never hurled. Philip Ryan was a farm labourer, born in Cooldine, Killenaule, in 1888. According to the 1911 census, Philip was one of six children born to James and Ellen Ryan. All the men in the family worked as labourers, while Ellen was a housekeeper and Philip's sister, Margaret, worked as a domestic servant for one of the gentry families who lived in the area.

Across the road from Jimmy's house is a GAA pitch, which the late Canon Kelly bought for the local GAA club in the 1950s. 'I saw lads thinning beet in that field when I was a young lad,' he recalls. 'On wet days, sacks around their knees, creeping along the drills, thinning it, pulling out the surplus by hand so there'd be enough room for the roots to develop.'

Jimmy and his friends subsequently paced out the pitch and helped raise enough money to erect a stone wall around the perimeter, which was built by the late Paddy Fitzgerald and the late George Lyons. They also installed a gate and a stile at the entrance. A stonecutter called Brophy was paid ten shillings to cut two stones out for the gate piers. Of his own volition, Mr Brophy cut one in the shape of Bill Casey, the Mayo footballer, and the other for Tommy Doyle, the Tipperary hurler. 'They called Tommy Doyle "the Rubber Man" because he was so fit,' says Jimmy. 'He was the only man to hold Christy Ring scoreless for two games.'

Although he's under time pressure, Jimmy insists there is time enough to make a hurley. We listen to the zings and zims of bandsaws and lathes as he crafts a fresh one, spinning it around in his hand, feeling for lumps and bumps. The coarse sander, the fine sander, the sawdust cones piling high. It is a good thing he wears a dust mask, as well as his blue coat and hat.

While he's sanding, Jimmy talks of his passion for greyhounds. 'I go to the dogs on a Thursday or a Saturday night. I'm only a very small-time gambler, but I like looking at the dogs and I enjoy the craic with my doggy friends, and my GAA friends too. In the past two years, eleven of the lads I go to the greyhounds with have gone. Sometimes I'd be thinking, *Ryan, are you next?*'

As he finishes making the new hurley, two knee-high grandsons rush into the room, wielding small hurleys. 'Hup-ho!' cries Jimmy, delighted. 'Would you look at those men with the hurleys! It all starts with a little lad and a small hurley.'

Joe Waldron & Brendan Drewett

Naas, County Kildare

Painter & Boxer and Cotton Mills Fitter

Born 1933 & 1933

'I do the Lucky 15 every day,' says Joe Waldron. 'It's something to do in the morning. Walk down, look at the papers, write out my Lucky 15, go home and wait for the results.'

'I never had a bit of luck on horses,' says Brendan Drewett, shaking his head solemnly.

'Me neither,' retorts Joe, 'but one day! It's only fifteen cents each way. And if it does come in …'

'It's a madman's game,' continues Brendan. 'I don't back them at all.'

'… well, then, winner all right, says I,' finishes Joe.

Brendan and Joe have been friends all their lives, perpetually bonded by the dual coincidence of age (they were both born in 1933) and education (they attended the same school in Naas).

'There were three of us that were friends at school,' says Brendan. 'Myself, Joe and another lad, Donal Reid, who lives in England now. Figgy 1, Figgy 2 and Figgy 3. That's what they called us.'

Joseph Drewett, Brendan's grandfather, was a Catholic Englishman who worked as a warehouse foreman in Dublin for the British army before independence. With the advent of the Irish Free State, Brendan's father, Ernest, found work as an accountant for the Irish army at the Curragh Camp.

But the maths that most interested Brendan as a young man was simply the countdown from ten to one whenever he felled one of his boxing opponents.

'I was bantamweight,' says he. 'I had a few auld boxes in The Towers on the Fair Green in Naas. It was a workman's club where the Kildare footballers would meet years ago. I was sixteen when I stepped into the ring and I boxed for nearly four years. I got plenty of wallops, I can tell you, but there were a few lads taken away off the pitch too.'

By the time he was twenty, Brendan was working as a fitter at the Naas Cotton Mills. Assigned to the nightshift, he was unable to keep up his boxing. 'I always kept fit though,' he says. 'I used to do a lot of walking and running, maybe ten miles in a day, with the dogs, going off to get rabbits.'

When he started at the cotton mills, Joe Waldron was with him. 'I went into the mill from school when I was fourteen years of age,' says Joe. 'I stayed two years and then I served my time as a painter after that.'

Joe's grandfather, William Waldron, was a slater but his father, Samuel, had branched out and become a

painter. Colouring and whitewashing the walls of the town and surrounding countryside enabled Samuel to bring home enough money to look after nine children born in nine years, of whom Joe was the second oldest.

Joe's penchant for a flutter is understandable given that the house where he grew up was only a mile and a half from the Punchestown racetrack. (In later life, Joe secured the contract to paint the grandstand.) Not only that, but his bedroom window overlooked a field that doubled as the town's greyhound track for many a long year.

For Brendan, the greatest change in the area has been the influx of new people to Naas which has seen its population rocket past 26,000. There's a lot of talk about just how big the population of Naas was back in the 1950s. Some reckon it was over 5,000, others put it nearer 3,000. Brendan pegs it at 1,800. But all the statisticians agree that the population was a whole lot smaller and that, not so long ago, everyone knew everyone else.

Many of those with whom Brendan and Joe were at school subsequently emigrated to England. The last of Brendan's brothers and sisters crossed the Irish Sea when the cotton mills closed in 1970. Brendan toyed with the idea of leaving while he worked part time as a barman in Naas but then found work at the ESB power station in Allenwood.

So between the emigration and the newcomers, the old sense of intimacy in Naas is long gone. It's not all gloom and doom though. 'All I have to do now is look along the pavements for someone with grey hair and I'll find someone I know,' says Brendan.

Both men are married. Joe was first to wed back in 1962, and he has a son and a daughter. Brendan held out on his own until he was thirty-nine and is now the father of five.

As our talk comes to an end, I can tell that Joe is itching to find out how his Lucky 15 fared. I suspect that Brendan might even ride along to the bookies with him, just to see whether today's the day that Figgy 2 comes up trumps.

Coleman Coyne & Máirtín Joyce

Connemara, County Galway

Fisherman and Seaweed Harvester & Fisherman, Factory Worker and Oarsman

Born 1925 & 1931

'I swim like a rock,' confesses Máirtín Joyce. 'I had an uncle on my mother's side who was a great swimmer but, even though I was born on the edge of the sea, I would be afraid to swim like that.'

Coleman Coyne is the very same. In fact, most of the old fishermen and sailors along Ireland's west coast were unable to swim.

Not that it stopped them living their life at sea. Take Máirtín, for instance. Together with two of his Joyce cousins, he won the All-Ireland rowing championship four times in the 1950s and early 1960s, three of them consecutively, as well as the Galway county championship a staggering six times in a row.

'It was good going,' he acknowledges quietly.

'Máirtín Joyce is a tough man,' asserts Coleman, who rowed with him on many occasions. 'He's the strongest I ever met. That's the God's truth. And it was very near killing me to keep up with him. Rowing, rowing, rowing.'

The two men have known each other since childhood when they grew up on the neighbouring islands of Illauneeragh and Inishbarra on the east side of Kilkieran Bay off the south Galway coast.

Given that Máirtín is in his eighties, you'd have thought his rowing days might be behind him. Not at all. Granted, he's presently residing in his cottage 'on the mainland', waiting for a new hip to settle in, but the moment it does, he'll be hauling his boat back out onto the water and rowing back to Inishbarra, the island where he was born and raised.

Inishbarra is a lofty, rocky, heather-clad, five-hundred-acre island, blessed with a beautiful clean sandy beach that was created on its western side by a storm.

The 1911 census records one hundred and forty-seven residents on the island, mostly cottier farmers, with the occasional carpenter and boat builder. The Joyces have been here ever since Máirtín's great-grandfather, Patrick Joyce, came down from the mountains during the Famine to live near the shore.

'There was a lot of shellfish and every kind of fish around the island at that time,' says Máirtín. 'And there was a lot of turf on the island then, but there's no sod of turf there now. They sold the turf to the Aran Islands so it was all gone out when I was growing up.'

Opposite page: Coleman Coyne.

When Máirtín was born, there were still sixteen families on the island. He recalls a lot of activity on the island in his childhood years, with much music and dancing in the family kitchen. By 1954, several families had relocated to County Meath, leaving just nine families on the island. When his friend John William Seoige left in 1964 there were only four. His father died in 1979 and Máirtín has been on his own on the island since 1983.

'Down and down it went until I was the last. You'd think it would be strange to be on your own but, when you get used to it, you wouldn't take any notice of it at all.'

His grandfather and his father came from large families but, in both instances, all of their siblings emigrated to America. One of his aunts, his godmother, was dispatched as a nun to Africa. 'She stayed there for a long time because she wasn't allowed to come home, not even when her mother died. It was a hard rule, very strict. But she did come home in the end and she died down in the convent in Tralee.'

Emigration prevailed again for Máirtín's siblings. Aside from two sisters who died of meningitis and pneumonia in their teens, he had two sisters in Pittsburgh, another in New Hampshire and a brother in Boston. He visited the USA in later life and mused about staying but ultimately concluded that emigration was a young man's game.

He was a part-time emigrant, mind you. When he was seventeen years old, he and some friends were cycling in from the bog at Costello when they met an agent from a sugar factory in England who was looking for workers. Máirtín told the agent he was twenty years old and, the next thing he knew, he had a full-time job at a factory in King's Lynn on the coast of Norfolk.

'We were given the hardest job because we were the youngest,' says he. 'It was so hard, you had to be very strong. And so hot that I couldn't even wear a singlet. I'd have a towel tied around my belt to catch the sweat.'

He spent the next seven seasons in England, either working in the sugar factory or pulling beet and picking potatoes for a farmer in Yorkshire. Such physical labour ensured he was in peak condition when he got back home to help his father with the farm. They lived in a sturdy, slated house that had been constructed by his father in 1924. It was built with rock from a nearby quarry and the stones from the original thatched cottage where Patrick Joyce had lived seventy years earlier.

Coleman Coyne's family lived in a similar abode on Illauneeragh, a Coyne stronghold since the mid-nineteenth century. He empathises with Máirtín's defiant stance on Inishbarra because his family were the last to leave Illauneeragh. 'We left the island in 1951 because it was too hard going,' he says. 'We were the one year there on our own and we were very near gone cracked.'

Coleman felt trapped on the island by the unpredictable seas. 'Not being able to get out, that was the worst of it.' On the plus side, if the water was too rough, he didn't have to get in his boat and row over to school on Inishbarra. When he was of an age, Coleman went to London to work on a building site but he decided England was not for him. Instead, he returned to Connemara to trawl the waters for winter mackerel, herring and whitefish.

'We had to be fit then because we were rowing every day from the islands,' explains Máirtín. 'When you go out to the shop, you have to row in and out. Or to the post office in Lettermore or to mass. It doesn't matter where you go, you had to row. And maybe the tide would be for you or maybe it would be against you going out and against you coming in.'

When he wasn't racing, Máirtín was either harvesting seaweed or looking after his father's cattle, primarily Angus, Hereford, Limousin and Strawberrys. The cattle generally came and went to the island via a rocky causeway, constructed in 1847, which appears at low tide to connect several islets. Sometimes, they transported them by boat but that could be a troublesome business. Unless each cow is securely roped in, 'they wouldn't be long jumping out'.

Opposite page: Máirtín Joyce.

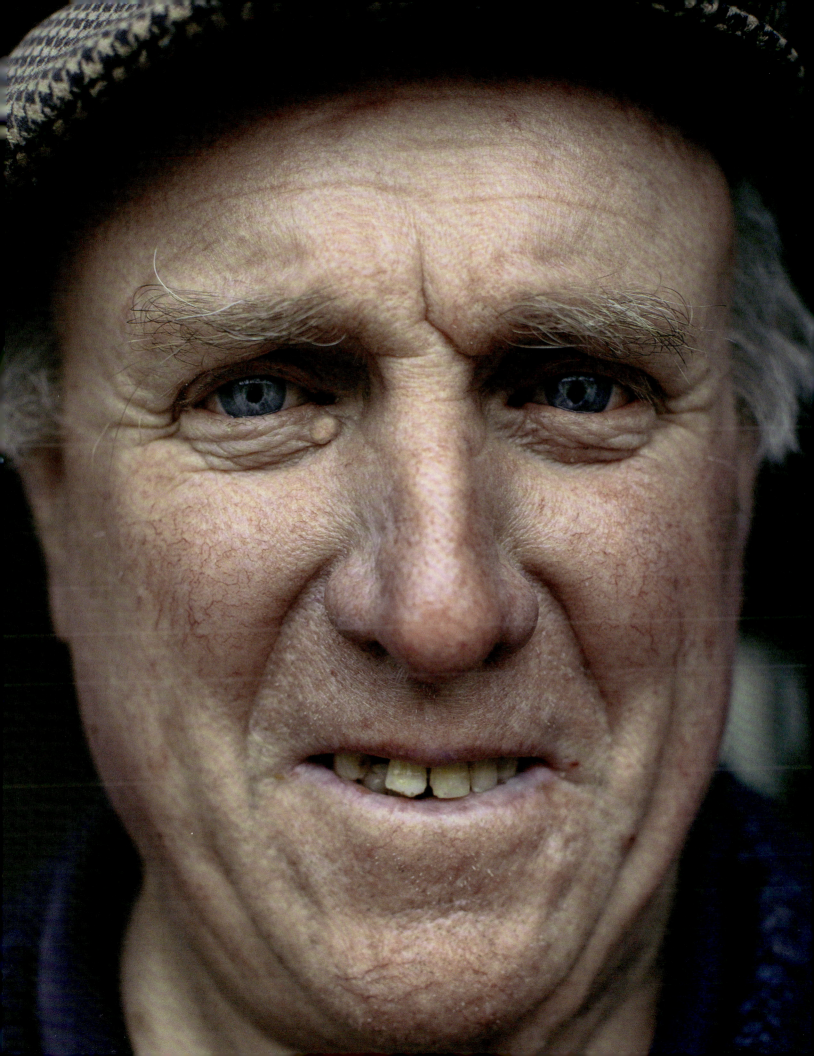

Máirtín never married and is perfectly content on his own. On the 'mainland', he sometimes stays in the house he built with his own hands five decades ago as a holiday home for his sisters in case any of them returned from America for a visit. He is also a skilled builder of traditional boats, both great and small. When we visited, he was working on a model of a Galway hooker which he planned to give to a friend from Kilkenny who visited him frequently in hospital.

He is longing to return to Inishbarra although he concedes it is not as easy as it once was. 'It's not the same island now as it was when I was growing up. It was very clean at the time because the people were sowing potatoes and oats and everything. But now, it's gone wild with the briars and the blackthorn. It doesn't take long to go wild.'

In 1956, Coleman Coyne married Bríd Ridge, who worked in the Carna knitting industry. She not only knitted him a fine collection of woolly jumpers and cardigans, but she also became mother of his ten children, all of whom now live in Ireland bar one son in Boston. 'I was in Boston once and I spoke more Irish in it than I do here in Galway,' laughs Bríd. 'Some of the accents you hear in Boston would be stronger than anything you would hear in Ireland now.'

The Coynes live in the village of Kilkieran, close to the seaweed factory where their son, Michael, now works. Coleman has hauled plenty of seaweed to the factory since it opened in 1947 and worked there on and off over the years. Out at sea, he would source a good crop of seaweed, cut it, hoop it, tie a rope through it and bring it on in.

Coleman does not think about the islands as much as he used to. 'They're all dead and buried now,' says he of the men with whom he used to fish. 'I am so happy out here,' he says of his present life. 'My dancing days are over but I really am happy.'

But I would bet that when he closes his eyes, he can still hear the shanties echoing across the water, the synchronised splash of a currach's oars, the skitter of a crab across the rock pools of Illauneeragh, the soft sandy beach on the island's shore where he and his young brothers would lie on sunny days when all the world was a little younger.

Tom Sheehan

Kilbaha, Moyvane, County Kerry

Schoolteacher and Actor

Born 1931

'I doubt if anyone enjoyed school in those days,' muses Tom Sheehan, puffing on his pipe. 'It was a time of corporal punishment. But, unfortunately, children were punished – not for bad behaviour, but for failure at lessons. It wasn't Ireland alone though. The same thing was happening in England and Wales. Have you ever read *How Green Was My Valley*? It's terrible what went on. But I was okay really. I got off lightly in comparison with some.'

Given that Tom endured rather than enjoyed his school years, you might not have expected him to become a schoolteacher, but that is precisely what he did when he left school in 1949, relocating from his native Kerry to faraway County Cavan.

Teaching was not in his blood, but emigration was. Dick Sheehan, his father, was a farm labourer who spent most of Tom's early years in England.

'Things were very tough in the early thirties,' explains Tom. 'Money was so scarce, even in England. My father was in his mid-twenties when he got married. He needed to gather up the price of a house, so he went to England with two of his brothers and they worked with a big dairy farmer in Surrey. They supplied milk to London. I was only a year old when he went and I don't think he came home again for two or three years.'

Dick and his brothers were not the first Sheehan family members to emigrate. Four of their aunts and uncles had moved to Kansas before the First World War. Tom's mother, Peggy, also knew the tug of foreign lands as two of her aunts had settled in Chicago. 'At that time, people going to America practically had to be adopted by someone who could guarantee their family,' says Tom.

While Dick was earning money in England, Tom was raised in the parish of Murhur by Peggy and her mother, Mrs Thornton. They lived about half a mile away from Tom's present home, which Dick built after his return to Ireland in 1934.

'Himself and a friend built a house for the friend the first year. And the next year, they built this house. It was a full-time job and took them most of a year to build. It happened to be a very bad autumn, winter and spring and I can remember mud everywhere. They got the material from Listowel but the sand had to be drawn from rivers, and it was very poor quality. The land here is very heavy, so in wet weather you can imagine the amount of mud. They had to draw rushes in to soak it all up. There was no tractors then, so I'd imagine they borrowed a horse to draw them.'

Fortunately, it has proved a sturdy dwelling. 'There was a number of houses built around here that time,' says Tom. 'I think there was a grant of £100 going, when wages were about £1 a week. An old cousin of mine told me years ago that this was the only one of those houses still standing fifty years on, because the others were so poorly built.'

Tom, the eldest of six children, was initially schooled at nearby Kilbaha. He then went to St Patrick's secondary school in Glin and, during the week, he stayed with his aunt Kitty and her husband, Jack Adams, the Glin blacksmith. While at St Patrick's, he realised that it wasn't just the teachers who used violence on children. 'We were playing ball at school once. There was a fellow with a purple and blue line up his back and along his side. He said he had been walking on top of a gate, a tightrope sort of thing, and that he fell. That evening we were walking home and he said, "I didn't fall on the gate at all. It was my dad that beat me."'

Fortunately, Tom's parents refrained from such violence. 'I was very fortunate,' he says. 'I was never slapped by my parents. My mother hit me with a wet towel once but I never held it against her. My father was very strict but he never slapped us.'

By the close of the Second World War, Dick and Peggy were operating a general grocery shop from their home and Tom would cycle back from Glin at weekends to help them run it. 'All the sugar and tea had to be weighed,' he recalls. 'Every pound counted and there were 240 pennies in a pound in those days.'

'Life was a struggle,' says Tom. 'I was looking through memoriam cards recently and I would say that nine-tenths of the people who died when I was growing up were between fifty and seventy.'

Tom left school at the age of eighteen and went to Dublin to spend two years training to be a teacher at St Patrick's College in Drumcondra. After a few months working at the Model School on Dublin's Marlborough Street, he was asked to take a job in County Cavan.

'It was in a remote, poor area of Cavan called Knockbride, near Bailieborough. I went there on a miserable, cold November evening. I didn't expect to stay long. I hoped I would have a job in Kerry before Christmas. But it was very hard to get jobs that time and, well, I retired from there thirty-seven years later.'

Tom taught 'everything', primarily to children aged between nine and eleven. Sometimes, he felt very far away from his Kerry homeland, not least with the Troubles in full flow along the border. 'I was in Cavan when all the bombing and shootings was going on in the North. At least once a week, we could hear the booms of bombing going off twenty or thirty miles away. You had to be careful about where and when you travelled. But *sin scéal eile*, that's another story.'

Away from the classroom, Tom turned his mind to theatrical matters. 'Amateur dramatics came into a lot of country places in those times,' he recalls. 'I was part of a group called the Pavilion Players. Sometimes, I was producing but I was mostly acting or working as a make-up artist. I think my favourite role was playing one of the brothers in Joseph Tomelty's play *All Souls' Night*. We played at many drama festivals – Cavan, Bundoran, Navan, Dundalk and several others. There was an All-Ireland final every year in Athlone. We got into the final twice and we came third in the rural section one year.'

Every summer holiday, he returned to Kerry to help his parents run the shop and gather in the turf. In 1975, Dick and Peggy closed down the grocery. Such home enterprises were already starting to feel the squeeze of the supermarkets, though Tom attributes their retirement to old age. Dick died three years later, aged seventy-three.

Tom himself retired from Cavan in 1989. 'It was earlier than I intended to retire but my mother was living on her own and she was not very well. So I returned here. I had an idea of returning to teaching but it did not happen.'

He also devoted a good deal of his spare time to his twin pastimes of photography, with an old box camera, and fishing. 'I had my own boat on the lakes in Cavan but the thing I looked forward to mostly was coming back down here to fish on the river. I would always be looking forward to that.'

Kathleen Doyle & Jackie Bracken

Naas, County Kildare

Telephonist & Cobbler and Power Station Worker

Born 1930 & 1932

'I lived by the canal all those years but I was a dreadful swimmer. They never succeeded in teaching me. I knew what went into the canal, you see, and there was no way I was going to get into it.'

When Kathleen laughs, it has a Tinker Bell effect on everyone around her, making the air feel instantaneously young and vibrant. She is recalling her childhood on the banks of the Grand Canal, where she grew up with her father, Kildare footballing legend Jack Higgins, her mother, Molly, and her five younger siblings.

Jack made his debut for Kildare in 1925 and was to be the pride of the Lilywhites for a decade, during which time they brought home the Sam Maguire twice and won seven Leinster championships.

Such was his celebrity that whenever any boats came past his house, the Higgins children were invariably invited on board. 'They all knew my father so they'd give me and my brothers and my sister, Statia, Lord have mercy on her, a lift to the next bridge and we'd ride back.'

Living by the canal presented the occasional close call. One Sunday morning, the family were enjoying a canal-side stroll when her brother Frank – 'a lovely little red-head' – tumbled headlong into the reeds in his two-piece suit. Jack hastily dived to the rescue, clad in his Sunday best. 'But Frank became a fine swimmer after,' she chuckles. 'There was no getting away with it for him.'

One of her grandfathers was a gardener for the de Burgh family who lived in the fine mansion of Oldtown just outside Naas. Kathleen and her friends would sometimes slip into the demesne for a play when they were children. 'We were always very gentle and fairy-like,' she says. 'You respected places like that. We never even broke a twig.'

Her greatest delight was Irish dancing. 'We had so many magic nights in Lawlor's Ballroom,' she recalls. 'There were dances every other weekend, for the farmers, for the guards, for Christmas. Big dickie-tie jobs for the hunt and all. It was brilliant. I remember one time they fitted eighteen hundred people in for the Royal Showband. Mick Delahunty was the man of the time.'

The telephone network in Ireland was moving into the age when the postmistress and her underlings became the most knowledgeable members of the community. Kathleen joined their ranks at the age of sixteen, shortly after she left secondary school.

'I was the eldest, so I was the first to go out and get a job. I was a telephonist. I started in Naas, in the back of the post office, taking calls and going through the exchange. There was a big piece of wood in front of you and you had to stick a plug into a socket every time you wanted to make a connection. "Number please?" They were long days, eight hours at the switchboard with the odd cup of tea. You had headphones on all the time too, which would give you an earache, but you just had to get on because that was your job.'

After she completed her training in Naas, she was transferred to Arklow, which was 'lovely except for the smell of stale fish', and then went on to Bray where she lived a five-minute walk from the esplanade. 'I have had water by me all my life,' she says. 'I have a great love for the sea and water.'

In 1953, she married Cecil Doyle, a clerical officer with Kildare County Council who became one of the founding members of the Naas Credit Union. They have eight children who, all now married, have added Japanese, Italian and American in-laws to the Doyle–Higgins bloodlines. Kathleen and Cecil frequently holiday in Italy. The language barrier isn't a problem. 'Cecil learned enough Latin when he was an altar boy for us to get by,' says she.

Jack Higgins passed away in 1955 on account of the severe injuries he received to his back and spine during his footballing days. He was just fifty-three years old. Nearly six decades on, his daughter still misses him desperately. 'I had just been up to see Dad in hospital. We weren't talking to him or anything, just seeing him. And then later I was back at my aunt's house, listening to the news in Irish on the radio. And they announced that my father had died. It was so terribly sad.'

The Higgins' house stood a quarter of a mile away from the cottage of Jackie Bracken, who was arguably Jack Higgins' greatest fan. 'I have been closely involved with Kildare football for over sixty years and I've enjoyed every minute of it,' he says. His passion was undoubtedly stirred by the extraordinary success of Higgins and the Lilywhites in the 1920s and 1930s. In less than a minute, Jackie reels off the names and positions of every man who played for that team.

Jackie captained the Naas team which claimed victory in the County Junior Championship in 1952. The following year, the Naas under-eighteens won the County Minor Championship, again under Jackie's stewardship. He also played in the Kildare junior county team that was narrowly beaten by Monaghan in the All-Ireland final at Navan in 1956. Jackie served as a county board delegate representing Naas from 1948 to 1968. During that period, the greater struggle was not winning titles but watching his best players pack their bags and head off to new lives overseas, primarily in the big English cities of London, Birmingham and Manchester. 'Emigration was a constant,' says he.

The Brackens have lived in the same canal-side cottage at Abbey Bridge since at least the 1850s. Jackie's grandfather, Joseph Bracken, worked for Odlums. 'Every morning he'd set off on his rounds with a pair of draught horses, carrying eight bags of flour, one ton per dray, and he would go around distributing it in Blessington, Donard, Dunlavin and Baltinglass, and then home via Kilcullen.'

Joseph and his wife Marcella had ten children. One of their daughters, Katie Bracken, sailed for the USA in 1905 to start a new life as a nun and teacher but died of consumption as a young woman before the First World War.

Meanwhile, Jackie's father, also called Joseph, found work as an assistant in McDermott's hardware store in Naas. Joseph served with the Irish Republican Army in the War of Independence. During the ensuing Civil War, he was embroiled in an ambush of Free State troops at Ferrycarrig, County Wexford. Somebody hurled a hand-grenade into the back of the truck where he sat and, but for a mattress that lay between him and the blast, he would have been killed outright. He was nonetheless badly wounded and lost an eye.

In 1930, Joseph married Mary Coughlan from Glasson, County Westmeath, who worked as a domestic maid for some of the local dignitaries in Naas, such as the vet and the formidable parish priest, Father Doyle.

Born in the canal-side cottage at Abbey Bridge in 1932, Jackie was one of two children. It was a tiny family by comparison with their neighbours – the footballer Billy Kelly was one of eighteen children and the Sheridans had twenty-one.

'My mother didn't have time for a large family. She was let die with an appendix on 18 May 1940. That's a red-letter day in Abbey Bridge. She had my brother out at communion on the Saturday morning and she was rolling around in the bed all day. The doctor never came and she passed away that evening. She died in an ambulance as it crossed over the Abbey Bridge on its way to Dublin.'

In 1946, Jackie went to work in the slipper factory which stood beside the cotton mills. Eighteen months after he joined, the factory closed down. Fortunately Mr Tutty, the manager, started up a new shoe factory on Poplar Square beside Lawlor's Hotel.

'And I served my time in Tutty's then,' says Jackie. 'Making shoes and boots. Tutty had a van on the road at that time and we would go all around Kildare and Carlow collecting up shoes that needed to be mended.'

However, Jackie was unconvinced that his future lay in shoe repairs, not least because there were sixteen others on Mr Tutty's payroll and his chances of a promotion were consequently moderate to slim.

In the mid-1950s, the Electricity Supply Board and Bord na Móna teamed up to build a new power station on the Bog of Allen where turf could be converted into energy. The cooling tower that soared high above the bog remained an iconic Naas landmark until it was demolished in the 1990s.

Jackie decided to up sticks and start anew at the power station. 'When I told a friend what I had done, he said, "What kind of a gobshite are you? You're leaving a place where you're after serving your time!" I replied, "I am, but there might be more prospects where I'm going." Lo and behold, I was forty years in the ESB and I can tell you one thing, I made the right decision.'

Acknowledgments

With huge, all-encompassing thank yous to our beautiful brides, Ally Bunbury and Joanna Fennell, for their constant support and patience. And also to our miscellaneous young children – Bella Fennell, Jemima Bunbury, Mimi Fennell, Bay Bunbury and William Fennell – who, despite their youth, can already identify a Vanishing Ireland character at a hundred yards. These books are as much for our children and their generation as for anyone.

And thanks to Ciara Doorley for steering us through four volumes of Vanishing Ireland series with such tolerance and sagacity. Also to Claire Rourke, designer Karen Carty, Breda Purdue and all the team at Hachette Ireland, and Noelle Campbell Sharp and the Cill Rialaig Artists' Retreat.

And thanks also to the following for manifold assistance, both great and small, and moral support.

Susi Burton Allen, Alex and Daria Blackwell, Meike Blackwell, Alice Boyle, Ed Brennan, Michael Brennan, Nancy Brosnan (Stanley House), Donough Cahill (Irish Georgian Society), Alastair Hubert Bao Butler Crampton, John D'Alton (T.J. Newman's), Máirtín D'Alton, Philomena Daly, Lorraine Dormer, Annette Egan, Rory Everard, Vincent Fahy, David Fallon, Frank Farrell, William Fennell, Giana and Tom Ferguson (Gubbeen Farmhouse), Barnes Goulding, Patrick Guinness, Tom Halligan, Paula Hanley, Ann Hassett, Maureen Hegarty, Stan Hickey, Tom Horgan, Hugo Jellett, Arthur Johnson, Josie Keaney, Sue Kilbracken, Frank and Marianne Lawler, Alice Leahy, Gemma Lee, John McCartin, Ronan McGrath, Fiona McGrath, Helen McMahon (Mount Saint Joseph Abbey), Mary Monaghan (Monaghan's Harbour Hotel, Naas), Lisa Moore, Mick Moore, Miriam Moore, Margaret Moran, Mike Mullins, Liam Mulvaney, Bróna Murphy, Jasper Vincent Murphy (McCarthy's of Fethard), John Murphy, Mary Teresa Nee, Isabella Rose Faith Nolan, Derek O'Brien and Thalia Smithwick, Robert O'Byrne, William and Mary O'Keeffe, James O'Keeffe Lyons, Joan O'Leary, Thomas and Veronica O'Malley, Paul O'Meara (*Leinster Leader*), John Onions, Bernadette O'Shea, René Ostberg, Andy Philpott, Charlie Raben, Nicola Ronaghan, Paddy Ryan (St Gabriel's Hospital, Schull), Pádraig agus Cáitlín Seoighe, Jessica Slingsby, Sasha Sykes, Tom Sykes, Katie Theasby, Kitty Walsh, Alissa M. Zimman and the girls of Áras Éanna.